Getting Old

AND OTHER INDIGNITIES

DIANA EDEN

~~~~~~~~~~

Miranda Press

Praise for GETTING OLD AND OTHER INDIGNITIES

"A wonderful, funny and honest story of aging disgracefully, from an incredible woman who shatters stereotypes and reminds us that we hold the power to create our own adventures at any age."

~Carolyn Ray, CEO, JourneyWoman

GETTING OLD AND OTHER INDIGNITIES can transform the lives of the readers by influencing how they think about issues that most of us don't want to think about. The author will begin to feel like a personal friend who can tell you anything. You will laugh, and at times cry with her. You'll learn you're not alone in this stage of life called growing old.

~Holly James
Master Gunnery Sergeant USMC (Retired)

Diana's Eden captivating memoir, *Getting Old and Other Indignities*, helps you imagine creative alternatives to aging in sweat pants in front of reruns of "Name that Tune"—timely fashion, travel, new companions—even for those living alone, as 35% of women oven 65 are. *In short, it opens up choices for aging with agency.* She shows you the way, bringing you along step-by-step through her own re-invention after losing not only her previous job, but her much younger husband, his Sunday "sauce," local wines during their trips in the hill towns above the French Riviera and, not in any way the least, his touch.

Clear-eyed and honest even to the point of recognizing the "indignities" of plucking chin hairs, managing "roots," fending off bald blind dates, navigating financial fears, even conceding to wear sneakers on some overseas trips with steep stairs, Diana models how to handle it all with humor and grace. For the reader, no matter what age, it is a great trip.

~Judith Huge, Author
"A Middle Aged Woman and the Sea," a Traveler's Tale.
Co-author *101 Ways to Help: How to Offer Support and Comfort for Those Who Are Grieving*.

DEDICATION

For my sister Carol, one of the bravest people I know
and
For all my sons and daughters of the heart

CONTENTS

PREFACE

I first met Diana in 2020, when she wrote an article for me called 'Life Doesn't End at 80. Neither Does Travel". In it, she told the humorous story of her financial advisor relegating her to a rocking chair on her 80th birthday. "Not me!" she said. "I flat out refuse!" Since then, Diana has written almost 40 articles for JourneyWoman sharing her travel experiences on safaris, food tours, long-haul flights and of course, staying stylish while travelling.

To my pleasure, Diana has also joined me on stage at travel events to talk about 'traveling like a rock star' in her 80s. At one, the room erupted with applause when she closed her remarks with: "Eat the gelato. Check the bags. Buy the shoes. Take a nap. Sleep with the guitar player. Travel like a rock star." At another, she wasted no time getting to the heart of things on a panel in New York City—saying that one of the things that changes when you travel solo at age 80 is the frequency of orgasms and sex, which still makes me laugh to this day.

With Diana, there is no taboo topic. She likes nothing better than shattering a stereotype—and in her case, she does it with style and flair. In this, her second memoir, Diana shares a real, honest and sometimes raw take on her life and her many successes and lessons (and regrets). I admit to simultaneously laughing and crying as I read this book, knowing as I do what a warm and gentle heart she has and the grief she experienced losing her beloved husband Dominic so unexpectedly.

Above all, Diana reminds us that you are never alone—many of us share the same fears of isolation and self-doubt. However, her true gift is empowerment, reminding us that we have the power to make our own lives happen. A full and active life doesn't arrive quietly on your doorstep, you have to get out in the world and find it, just as she has done through her own example. I'm honoured and thrilled to call her a

I

friend (and fellow Canadian) and grateful to have her as a role model as I chart my own path to 'aging with indignity'! Bring it on!

- Carolyn Ray, CEO, JourneyWoman,
Toronto, Canada August 2025

INTRODUCTION

My husband Dominic

On April 1st, 2008, my husband and I pulled out of our Sherman Oaks, CA garage for the last time. I had the two cats with me in my car, and he had his car piled high with the last bits and pieces of our life there that had not already been shipped ahead. We each played our own music favorites at full volume as we headed up the I-15 to Las Vegas, our new retirement home. The cats, Sophia and Gina, yowled their indignation at being confined in their carrier for four hours on this highway to the unknown.

"Where on earth can we retire to?" Dominic had asked in an earlier conversation. "Well, it has to be warm, or I'm not going," I responded.

"What about Las Vegas? I've already worked there, and I know there will still be work part-time in the entertainment industry, should we want that."

Dominic was dubious.

"It has an international airport, and people will come visit us. People always love to come to Las Vegas", I persisted. That might have done it. Plus the fact that the cost of living is a fraction of what it is in Los Angeles, and we can buy a brand-new house for cash and "live like kings!". Mission accomplished. Vegas it was.

Before I retired, my typical day at work designing the costumes for NBC's "Passions" was about ten to twelve hours long, busy, exciting, and full of lively interactions with actors, directors, costume crew, stage crew, production crew and shop owners. Literally dozens of people of all types crossed my path each day. The pace was frenetic, but it was exhilarating. It was fun. I felt confident in my costume design abilities, and in my way of dealing with actors, and teammates. More importantly I felt valued. I was in my element, in my happy place, feeling the power of being part of the amazing Hollywood entertainment industry

CUT! Retirement is here.

My official last day on NBC's daytime drama "Passions" was a Friday, and it was also the show's last day after a run of eight years, five of them with me as Costume Designer. We had been cancelled by the network. At the good-bye party on Friday night, many friends came and wished us luck in our new Las Vegas adventure. On Saturday, my husband and I ran around doing final errands, and Sunday morning we backed our cars out of the garage and headed to Las Vegas. It felt like the highway to oblivion. What was ahead for us? How would retirement feel?

Once we arrived, Sophia and Gina adjusted far quicker than we expected. Not traumatized or cowering under the bed in a strange new bedroom, they peeked out from their confines, took a look around, and decided this didn't look too bad.

"This will do just fine, thank you very much." said Sophia.

I wasn't so sure.

We had to deal with a house with no window coverings, new furniture still on a boat from China, and boxes and boxes full of the stuff of our last twenty-eight years together—theatre programs, movie scripts and mementos, travel scrapbooks, boxes of pasta dishes and giant pots, and way too many clothes. Why would we need all this? On retiring, I thought death was near. I was in the cell phone parking lot waiting for the call. I was just going to putter around until it happened and hope it wasn't too long a wait. But the years to come would yield some surprising answers--- some enriching, some life-crushing and all unexpected. It turned out to be a new beginning, one requiring a massive re-invention of who I thought I was.

This is the story of my reinvention, what I lost and what I found as I navigated the years after leaving an active and gratifying career in Los Angeles. I am not an expert on becoming old, nor is my research deep and scholarly, but there has been loss, grief, renewal, travel, loneliness, back pain, laughs, friends, and lots more. Still, adventure and discovery are possible past the point when most people think we are ready to be put out to pasture. This is not a how-to book on retiring with plenty of money, perfect health, tropical cruises, and a lovely group of similarly aged friends all enjoying "active adult" activities. Rather, this is my story, of how I am living my life as a single woman growing older, looking through new lenses.

PART ONE

CHAPTER 1
RETIREMENT: Is That All There Is?

A few weeks into retirement in Las Vegas, I find myself sitting in a Starbucks inside Target, playing solitaire on my phone. The sound of Peggy Lee's "Is That All There Is" echoes through my brain.

I am suddenly without all the people I have seen almost daily for the last five years. I am missing that wonderful, frenzied structure, those costume fittings with my actors, those panicked calls to the set of my TV show for which I designed costumes for the past half a decade! Instead, I wake up to breakfast with my husband Dominic and then face an empty day ahead. Nothing on the schedule. It's like running into an unexpected glass wall. I am stunned, dazed, and disoriented. The rhythms of my body and mind have been dramatically altered. I am not used to this eventlessness. Where's my parking spot with my name on it?

I didn't want to retire when I did, but circumstances way above my pay grade made it necessary. The television networks were finding that the world of daytime dramas (also known as soap operas) was proving more expensive compared to game shows and talk shows. Those only require a backdrop, a sofa and chair, perhaps an end table with a plant on it, and a likable talk show host with guests who did not have to be paid but are lining up to come on the show. As one soap after another was being canceled in the mid-2000s, I knew we were also headed for the chopping block. I would be looking for a new job again.

During those five years designing for "Passions," while I grew minimally older, all the producers seemed to shrink to twenty- and thirty-year-olds. They didn't know who I was! How could that be? I'd been designing for more than twenty-five years for top-notch, night-time, network TV series, plus for films and dozens of pilots. I had three Emmy nominations to my name. The producers who *did* know me were retiring themselves. So, I gave in to the inevitable. I called my union, put in the paperwork for retirement, and Dominic and I started making plans.

Retirement, portrayed in the media as one big sunny vacation until death, was actually proving to be a series of doors I had to walk through in order to get to that Senior Sandals Resort.

The first door we walked through was a change of location. Dominic and I had lived in the San Fernando Valley for thirty-eight years, in three different houses, all in the same neighborhood of Sherman Oaks, an area of Los Angeles tucked in to the side of the Hollywood Hills. Now we were moving to a city in the Nevada desert.

Our last house in LA was up a small, wooded canyon, less than five minutes from busy Ventura Boulevard, but miles away in the feeling of quiet and privacy. I'd miss the view from our front deck to the valley beyond, glimpsed through the branches of the very old oak tree right across the street from us. I'd miss the large pots of roses that produced masses of lovely blooms most of the year, despite my major lack of gardening skills. I'd miss the deer that wandered onto the hill just beyond our back wall and grazed there, then sometimes pull their legs underneath them to have a sit. I was amazed we could be in the middle of a big city and still have wildlife visit us.

I'd miss the jacaranda trees in June that turned Dixie Canyon into an arched purple passageway. I'd miss the fuchsia bougainvillea that spilled over walls all summer. I'd miss the little windy road that snaked down to our local grocery store, Mrs. Gooch's, in the triangle where Sepulveda Boulevard met Ventura, opposite the famous Sherman Oaks Galleria. Oh, the safety of sameness, the comfort of familiarity. But we were going to the desert, the land of rock and cactus. Luckily, I've always felt an affinity for the desert. There is a wildness, a feeling of space and endless possibilities that speaks to me in the desert.

I liked to fantasize that our new house being built in the northeast part of the Las Vegas Valley is the first building on this small plot of land *ever*. I know Native Americans lived in the area, but was it likely they would have picked our lot right in the middle of the open space without the protection of a hill or a stream? No. I like to believe that only the wild animals have crossed our little plot until now. Our dusty swath of earth has been here for eons and eons, long before the historians were around to describe it. Once covered by water, the winds whistle along its surface stirring up small beige wisps of sand. A long time ago, wooly mammoths wandered around here. More recently, coyotes, wolves, tortoises, rabbits, and many more animals scamper across our land. But no one built upon it. Until now. Us. Our new house. Our new life. I can't wait to walk through our new front door.

Our new house in the desert being built 2007

But another door I had to walk through left behind my identity as a busy costume designer for films and television in Hollywood. I missed the ritual of getting up and getting dressed in my smart pantsuit, putting on makeup and fixing my hair. I missed driving into the studio and seeing my showbusiness family of costume crew, actors, stage crew. Missing them, I languished upstairs on my sofa, took extended naps and mastered ways to procrastinate unpacking the various boxes of books and supplies.

One day, while online I decided to check out my profile on the Costume Designers Guild website. The CDG had been my union since 1983 and I served on every single committee they dreamed up, as well as serving two terms as Secretary and one as Vice President. But my profile was gone! Wiped off the map. Nowhere to be found. Talk about being ghosted, and by an organization I treasured. I've never felt so dismissed in my life. Totally invisible. Fortunately, a new president came in shortly after and a legacy section was formed and retirees re-instated on the website and treated to the respect we deserve.

Not shown in any retirement commercial either is how the new daily schedule for the retired people in question can also be an adjustment.

5

Dominic liked to watch TV at any time of the day and it drove me crazy! I must be the only American who doesn't Love Lucy. The sound of Desi's voice in the morning, calling Loooooo-cy and Lucy's fake baby crying, Waaaaa, when she didn't get her way set my teeth on edge. America's beloved TV couple were not mine! Not then. Besides "I Love Lucy," Dominic loved all Italian gangster shows and films, which meant we saw or listened to all the *Godfather* movies, *Scarface*, *The Bronx Tale*, *Casino* and *Goodfellas* at all hours of the day. The sound of gunfights shortly after breakfast is not my idea of a good start to the day. The cats hung out nearby, wondering what we were doing home all day.

"Why is there so much noise during our morning nap time? We usually have a quiet house to ourselves." said Gina to Sophia. *"I'm going to try the bedroom, where at least it's quiet and the bed smells familiar."*

Gina and Sophia stick close together

However, Dominic also liked to go off during the day to investigate grocery stores and test drive cars at some of the dealerships. From time to time, I would get a call from some poor salesman enquiring, "Has Mr. Calandra made a decision yet on the Mercedes (or Rav4 or Audi)?" Inner eye roll. We did continue our Sunday tradition established long ago in Los Angeles. We would have a late lie-in in bed, where Dom worked on a sudoku puzzle and I read the entertainment section of the paper. Then Dom would cook us an enormous breakfast of eggs, bacon, and potatoes. We'd select a movie to see. Sometimes, as we walked through a casino hand in hand, winding ourselves through the rows of gambling machines to the multiplex movie theaters, we would look at each other and say, "Can you believe we've moved to Las Vegas?" It felt very naughty and exotic. Soon, we began to make friends in our neighborhood, a community of 55-and-above retirees and near-retirees. We were invited to join a monthly dinner group called "The Ardiente Marching Band and Temperance Society," with events called, "Band Practice." Dominic's looks and wit made him a great "band member," and well, they got me, too. I could always entertain with stories of my days with Diana Ross or Betty White.

Dominic found work in our new town before I did. At my insistence (my usual role, The Pusher!), he went to an industry mixer where he learned of an audition the next day for "Tony n' Tina's Wedding," the interactive play that had been running since the 80s and now was at the Rio Hotel. He would be expected to present a monologue.

"You're a shoo-in for it," I told him, "You're Italian-American —— these are your people! You're a natural!"

So reluctantly, he went and, of course, was immediately cast. That began an eight-year run for him with the show, moving with it from hotel to hotel and forming a showbiz family that remains today as the "Tony n' Tina" family. I was so glad he had this connection.

He played several roles but was mostly featured as "Father Mark" who officiates the matrimonial ceremony between Tony and Tina and then proceeds to get progressively inebriated as the party goes on. He had such fun with it!

It took a bit longer for me to get work, but one day, I got a phone call from someone who had found me with an internet search and asked if I could make the blue gingham, Judy Garland pinafore from *The Wizard of Oz*. "Of course!" I said. We spoke a little longer, and I asked her for some basic sizes.

"I am large," she said.

"No problem," I said. "How tall are you?"

"About six feet," she answered. There was a pause. Then, she added, "Actually, I am a man."

*Dominic as Father Mark in "Tony n' Tina's Wedding". L to R Barbara
Lauren, Dominic, Maria Valdez. Ryan Flanigan*
Photo Credit: Joe Corcoran

Now, I paused, but only for a second. "No problem." We agreed on a price of $300 and that he would come to my house for measurements and bring a one-third deposit.

I am BACK! Right away, I felt a surge of energy and started looking at photos of Judy Garland in the dress. I had never examined its details before, the way the blue and white checks were on the bias on the straps and on the straight of grain on the skirt. The boxes still unpacked could wait. I had gingham to buy. On the day he was to come for measurements, he called me to say that he and his partner didn't have a car but would take a bus to the nearest intersection to me if I could come and pick them up. I agreed. So, I picked them up about two miles away, and they were not hard to spot. Matthew (not his real name) was indeed tall, plumpish, and blond, with a sweet impish face. His partner was small, muscular, and Hispanic. Easy to spot, for sure. Okay, so they weren't Scarlett Johannsen and Antonio Banderas, but they were *my* stars, and it was a start to my retirement career doing something I love. The joy this creation provided Matthew would make you think it was a bejeweled gown for Oscar night!

That's what made me happy to be doing this rather unusual project. I've always enjoyed and been rewarded for my hard work by the look of delight when a client, actor, or dancer sees themselves in the mirror for the first time, robed in their new outfit, a fulfillment of a fantasy of who they are or would like to be.

I had the first cut of the outfit ready quickly. What else would I be working on, for god's sake? Unpacking boxes when I could thankfully procrastinate again in favor of my artistic vision? However, Matthew told me it would be a while before he could save up for the second payment. Hmmm. Eventually, it was time for The Delivery, and once again, arrangements were complicated. Matthew told me they were in an apartment on the far northwest side of the valley and didn't know how they would get to me. Even though I knew I was extending myself further than was professionally necessary, I was committed by now and agreed to drive there with the dress. There was no answer to my knock when I arrived, but I heard agitated voices inside. Finally, Luis came to the door in tears and said their landlord was evicting them unless they came up with the final $200 of their rent. They had $100 (my last payment) and needed $100 more, which they thought they would have if they could get to an ATM. Was I out of my mind agreeing to help them? Maybe, but I needed to deliver the dress, and by now, I didn't even care about the last payment. I drove them to an ATM machine in pouring rain, and as we went from one ATM to another (they all seemed to be out of order), I thought how upset Dominic would be if he could see me driving around northwest Las Vegas in my car with two men, near-strangers, one in tears and one clinging to a blue gingham dress..

As odd as this scenario was, I was still glad that these two had brought me back to my sewing machine and jump-started my Las Vegas retirement career. Sixteen years later, I still worry about those two from time to time and wonder if they are Okay.

When I first retired, I vehemently resented the word retire with its etymology of "retreating, pulling back, withdrawing." It screamed at me all the things I didn't want—to relinquish engagement, to hold back, to be on the sidelines. This just felt so wrong for someone only 68 years old with a third of her life left to go. In fact, I was aghast when someone asked, "Are you retired?" You would have thought they'd asked me if I ate puppies for breakfast. I refused to acknowledge that I was retired, saying instead that I was continuing to work "part-time", according to my inclination. In other words, "elective employment." I hadn't thought of that term then, but it seems apt now, if somewhat elitist. And that's the thing. There is "work" and there is "a career." Work is the job that you do day in and day out to pay the bills and provide for yourself and your family what you believe is needed to exist and be happy. But a career that one loves? How can one just stop doing that? A role that is part of your daily life, your second family, your creative being. That is not something you can abandon quite as easily. The truth is, I missed my work enormously. The pundits never tell you how much you will miss everything about your former work life, and paint only the idyllic picture of an eternal vacation in some golden land.

We live much longer these days. In 1920, the average lifespan of an American was fifty-four years. Now it seems ninety years is the new norm. So, I do the math. A vast stretch of years spans between retirement in my late sixties and the expected frailty and loss of bodily functions I know are somewhere in my future. In fact, I have *several decades ahead*. I want to connect, contribute, and feel valued.

As I sat in Starbucks at Target, playing Solitaire, I wondered, "What have we done? Who is now my family? What lies ahead? Have we made a terrible mistake? "

No. I am not done. Not even close.

CHAPTER 2
TURNING SEVENTY: Do I Now Need to Pluck My Chin?

I don't remember much about my actual seventieth birthday, but I do remember that the number seven at the start of my age was a big wake-up call. When you are in your sixties you can say with some sense of ease, "I'm middle aged," though technically, that would indicate a really long life-expectancy, but you can get away with it. But with a seven at the front of your age, you have to admit you are at least old-ish. I never really expected to be this age - not sure that any of us do. It seems so far off when you are in your twenties and thirties, yet, here it is. Here I am. I hadn't much of a family example to follow. My mother died in her sixties, and my father's retirement from medicine at age seventy-one was an unwilling one, done because he realized his mini-stokes were affecting his ability to protect the safety of his patients. He died four years later.

After acknowledging I now was officially in another decade, I confess I felt and acted little differently from when I was sixty-nine. I enjoyed about a month of announcing my new decade to all who would listen, basking in their reaction of, "Seventy? No, you can't be!" but that got old soon. Nothing much changed in terms of my mental health, my bad habits, my good traits, my taste in vacations, my desire to work. I felt just the same. But looks? Right there in the mirror is a seventy-year-old. The wrinkles on the face are getting deeper, the marionette lines more pronounced. Oh, do I now need to pluck my chin? I never had hairs there before!

When people tell me I look young for my age, I confess I like it. But I am even happier when they say, "Your attitude is much younger than your age." I hope they are telling me that I still have curiosity, a sense of adventure and a desire to interact with the world outside my own small bubble of comfort. No one tells you exactly what a seventy-year-old is supposed to look like, or act like.

Like all women, I have been keeping an eye on my physical appearance for a long time now and cursing the gods for not allowing me to stay fresh and firm forever. Old-age creep is a challenge, but as my friend Ruth says, "We had our turn to be the hot ones."

We look at our faces every day in the mirror, first thing in the morning as we wash the sleep from our eyes, another look as we brush our teeth, a quick peak several times a day as we get ready to go out, a glance as we pass a mirror in the hallway or get ready to leave a public restroom, and then the last thing at night as we remove the vestiges of the day and add some night cream. Who hasn't taken both hands to the face and created an imaginary face lift? If only it were that easy!

As for my shape, two years into The Big R, retirement, I was already a size up from when I left Los Angeles. I hadn't completely let myself go in terms of food habits, but a less active lifestyle had added some weight. Damn! My size 6 dresses and pantsuits were straining to fit over a flabbier body. Taking stock, I find my silhouette still looks pretty good from the front, but turning sideways, I see the protruding belly. Where has my waist gone? How I miss it. I know it hasn't always been there, but it was there for a good long time, and I really enjoyed having it.

When I was about 3 1/2 and starting my ballet classes, a little girl in a pink leotard and pink tights I had a little potbelly. My potbelly was really, really cute then, totally adorable. As I grew into my 7, 8, 9, and 10-year-old body, I kept expanding out and up, but my torso was just one long skinny shape, a symphony of straight lines.. Perhaps around age 13, I developed breasts. I began to delight in my figure. In the throes of teenage narcissism, I confess I gazed into the mirror at the wonder of my beautiful shape. Those lovely curves from under the arms, in at the waist, and back out around the newly found womanly hips.

This was the time of 1950s fashions where styles accentuated the waist, the smaller the better. We sometimes wore waist cinchers and often wide, tight belts. Later came the sheath dresses of the '60s, and at that point, we were rather tired of being cinched in. In the 1970s, I joyfully bared my waist as I was living in sunny LA and wearing low-cut bellbottoms and crop tops.

But now my potbelly is back. I suck in and suck in and still no flat tummy. Damn! I know I must accept who I am and where I am, and yes, I do. Now I must wear dresses that skim discreetly over the offending protrusion.

In front of the mirror again I turn a little further and my crooked back and hip lump from scoliosis become evident. I don't look at my naked back much as it's tricky to twist to see it, but when I saw how large the hump on my right back hip has become from the curvature of my spine I was shocked. I saw a giant crease between the waist and the right hip, deep enough to hide a bear. On the left side there is a deep crease from shoulder to waist, reminding me of the sweeping lines in a heavily draped curtain, held back by a tie. Then the arms. One day in 2015 in Morocco, my sister took a photo of me. I was in super bright light, sunlight that shows *everything*, but I noticed in the photo how crepey my arms were. "Have they been like this long?" I asked. "Oh yes," she said. Shit.

And my long legs I was so proud of as a dancer, and which I believe helped gain me entry into the world of Broadway, were now a sorry excuse for the smooth and tight gams they once were. I'd known about the varicose veins on one leg for a while, but my doctor refuses to give me a referral to have them dealt with as they posed no medical danger and any operation or procedure would be purely for vanity reasons. Obviously, he's never worn a short skirt.

And then my hair. One day at the hairdresser, a woman came by the chair I sat in and asked my hairdresser, "Is she grey all over?"

"Oh no," I chimed in. "Just my roots."

Talk about self-denial!

So many women my age announce with great pride that they no longer wear makeup or dye their hair. For some women, going grey is empowering as a statement of self-acceptance. That's perfectly okay but the implication is that if you *do* dye your hair and paint your face, you are a narcissistic woman unable to process and accept the authentic, aging self. I challenge the notion that I am in denial of my age. I have always identified as a redhead. As soon as my first few hairs came in, late, according to my baby book, my hair was red, and my hair stayed red. Nor did I succumb as a teenager to experiments to die it purple or pink. My nickname was sometimes Big Red or Golden Girl or words to that effect so why would I change it? My dad's pet name for me was Gingernut.

Many years later, when someone had the nerve to point out that my roots were turning gray, without hesitation, I went to a colorist who figured out the perfect formula for me. I've been using that exact formula ever since. Now I go every five weeks for "Cut and Color" and I love the feeling of renewal and pampering I get at the beauty salon. I can almost fall asleep when my head is back in the sink and Jackie is washing my hair and massaging my scalp. What greater pleasure than this? And what greater pleasure to return home and have Dominic hug me and run his hands through my hair, saying "my redhead is back!"

Of course, I reserve the right to change my mind. I have worn a grey wig on two occasions when I played "an old lady" in films. Neither time did I recognize myself. Perhaps down the road?

The same thing goes with makeup. Why is it considered inauthentic to wear makeup after a certain age? I've always loved putting on makeup. Yes, I really enjoy the process. I would no more go out for the day without makeup than go out without brushing my teeth and combing my hair. The truth is, I didn't start to feel attractive until I started wearing a little mascara and lipstick. As a fourteen-year-old, I had never used any make up whatsoever, coming as I did from my culturally conservative, Canadian background. I had just turned fifteen-years-old, when I was hired to join the National Ballet Company of Canada for performances of Swan Lake at the Carter Barron Amphitheater in Washington DC. In the theater, artifice is everything!

Sitting at my dressing table backstage, one or two of the older dancers around me taught me the magic of stage makeup, a discovery of enormous significance. First, we started with the panstick base which, to my amazement, covered my skin with the smooth, even finish of a porcelain doll, not a blemish or a freckle to be seen. Next came rouge to give me a little color on the cheeks and suggest the look of fabulous high cheekbones. We had to paint eyebrows on since mine have always been completely blonde. Exciting! A face is emerging like a foggy image coming into focus through a camera lens.

Most exciting of all was painting my eyes. I was able to not only outline them, so people could see them, but extend those lines to make them bigger and bigger. The dancers also taught me how to melt a little black wax on a spoon over a candle and then apply it to my ever-so-blond eyelashes, forming a little black ball at the end of each lash. That was beyond all imagination… to be able to paint brand new eyes over the top of my own and make them double the size. My face transformed from a plain duckling into a beautiful swan, and dressed in my white tutu, I now could enter on stage an entirely new being. What's not to love about that?

*My friend Christina Ghiardi from the Nevada Ballet Company
demonstrates one kind of ballet makeup*

I continued to enjoy this pre-performance ritual. Later, on Broadway, in the dressing rooms shared with three to four other dancers, I was able to transform my face from something fairly pale and bland into something exotic and glamorous. This shared period of preparation was also one of bonding with my fellow performers, some of whom I still have lunch with sixty years later. I still like putting on makeup.

To this day, I do my makeup sitting down, as if at a theatrical style dressing table. I have my little vanity table with a mirror outlined with lights. I just can't put on makeup standing in the bathroom and leaning over a sink at a forty-five-degree angle. But that could also be because of myopia! In the mid-1960's, when I was an actress, I learned even more about cosmetics for everyday wear. It was also the era of extreme eye makeup. I, like the super model, Veruschka, painted a white strip and then a black line above my eyes, halfway from lid to brow. I emulated the 1960's icon Twiggy with her painted lower eyelashes. I went home to Toronto to visit my family one time sporting my "Twiggies" and got comments from my father. about "warpaint". Warpaint, indeed!

Me with actor Ted Reid in my dressing room at the
Blackstone Theater for "The Odd Couple"

Me in my warpaint!
Photo by Stan Malinowski

No, I am not the old lady with flaming orange hair, too much blue eyeshadow, and painted eyebrows with lines slightly off-kilter. Nor am I obsessive about creams, jellies, moisturizers, concealers, bases and all manner of colored pencils. I do not hang out at Sephora several times a week. My makeup purchases are usually made at CVS or a similar pharmacy chain and are inexpensive products such as Revlon and L'Oreal. My total cosmetic budget for the year is probably around $200. But I still enjoy my ritual of a light makeup before facing my adoring public.

If that means I am being vain and shallow, so be it. After all, I am seventy and hanging in there!

CHAPTER 3
MY EARLY 70S Professor Eden and
Then a Full Circle Experience

The biggest new thing to come into my life was the opportunity to teach costume design at UNLV, the University of Nevada, Las Vegas.

It started with an introduction to Judy Ryerson, Associate Professor, Theater, and Resident Costume Designer, who then introduced me to Francisco Menendez, who created the film department program in 1990. Judy asked me to give a forty-minute presentation on costume design to her theater students.

"But Judy," I said, "I have no idea how to teach. I've never done anything like this before. My training in costume design has never been academic."

"You'll be fine." said Judy. "Just talk about what you know."

Everything I knew I learned from watching Bob Mackie, whom I assisted for two years at the beginning of my costume career, and then Pete Menefee, whom I also assisted for nearly five years. I assisted both of them in the 1980's for their design of the Las Vegas showgirl extravaganza, "Jubilee," which played in Las Vegas for thirty-three years. I couldn't have asked for a better education in the world of costume nor asked for better mentors.

I had to really think through the process of what I had been doing by instinct for the last thirty years. Could I describe a 16th century farthingale? Or even know what one is? *No*. But what I did know was what it was like to show up on the first day of rehearsals of a new TV show or film, meet the actors, and start shopping and creating clothing for them. I could do this and meet not only their needs as performers, but do it within the producers' budget, and within the time frame required.

With this experience and knowledge behind me, I gradually mapped out what I would teach. What is the difference between fashion and costume? What is the difference between theater costuming and film costuming? How do I figure out what is in the script and what I must produce in short order? Whose approval do I need? How many people can I hire? Where will all this prep work take place?

In fact, where the hell do I start?

As I worked through this, I found there was a lot I could teach. I started to spend more and more time with the UNLV students and do more presentations in the film department. I always felt that designing for *film*, rather than for theater, was an under-represented area of study and I wanted to develop that. I started to build a course that would be specific to that need.

Apparently, the film department liked what they were seeing as in 2012, I was asked to design for a full-length feature film, *Stealing Las Vegas,* that was to be a co-curricular film at UNLV. In other words, it would be financed and produced professionally but crewed by students under the leadership of professional department heads. That's where I came in.

I arrived at my first production meeting, which turned out to be in a classroom, and learned two things: that the star would be Eric Roberts, an actor of some note, and yes, Julia Robert's brother. Secondly, my assistant would be a shy young girl in the film class with no experience on set other than student films, but with, she assured me, a knack for finding the best deals when shopping on a low budget.

Amber turned out to be a fabulous costumer. I showed her how to do fittings, keep copious notes, and track what's known as costume "continuity". She soon graduated from UNLV and became my assistant on many of the low-budget films I was hired for, becoming so valuable to me for her on-set and shopping skills that I didn't want to accept a job until I knew she could also be hired for it.

Working on a film within the university system had its trials. One was the petty cash issue. I refused to run around shopping for costumes using my own money in the hopes and expectations of being reimbursed eventually, so I was sent to the film department's "money man". We did not get along. He would give me $100, expect me to bring him exactly $100 worth of receipts for purchases before he would give me another $100.

"That's not the way it works," I would cry out in exasperation. "Everything is in flux until I fit the actors, choose their wardrobe out of the many choices I bring in, return the unused pieces to the store, and do some bookkeeping." There was no way I could turn in receipts ahead of time every few days! Welcome to Academia.

I was getting to know the Artistic Director of the film program, Francisco Menendez, who was to become a close friend, employer, colleague and more, and was co-writer and director on this film. He really listened to me, as he knew I came with a bag-load of experience. After one such explosion of frustration on my part about the petty cash situation, he handed over a personal check for $1000 so I could continue the work, knowing it would be safe in my hands. Another time he listened when I insisted I needed to go to Los Angeles to fit Eric Roberts and the four other principal players who lived there. This ruffled a few feathers in the department. "Who was this high-and-mighty ex-Hollywood person anyway? All these damned demands!"

"This is not a student production," I told Francisco, "where the cast shows up on the first day of shooting and you just figure out what they will wear then."

Eric Roberts and me. Friends by the end.
Photo by Amber Thomson

So, Amber and I were allowed to load up my car and drive to LA, check into the Sportsman's Lodge, and set up fittings for four of the leading players. We also had a lunch and private fitting with Eric Roberts at his house in Sherman Oaks, including Francisco and his writing partner and producer, Warren Cobb. They were able to see me as a professional at work. Eric did what many actors do on their first meeting… he tested me to see how much he could get away with. But it didn't faze me a bit. I took notes. "You want a pearl stick pin?" I asked. "No problem. You want your special kind of socks? Just give the name of them and where I can find them. You want a tie bar? Silver jewelry? I can do that."

To be sure, I was able to give him all those things (some of them after a raid on Dominic's closet) except the socks. I shopped and shopped for those damn socks and could not find them anywhere. I finally told him on the first day of shooting, "I can't find your socks, but here are four other options that are close. Choose one of them."

Antonio Fargas plays "Mo" in "Stealing Las Vegas".
Photo by Amber Thomson

My experience also showed itself when we went to the house of Antonio Fargas, a lovely man whom I remembered from his iconic role as Huggy Bear in the 1970s TV series, *Starsky and Hutch*. I had had discussions with Francisco about his character's look, that of a low-level manager in the basement of the casino in question, wielding power over the janitorial staff. But Antonio is a unique man and a unique actor, and he showed me various outfits of his own that he could use and lots of very exotic pieces of jewelry. I was able to step back and trust him rather than force my design ideas on him, which I might have done as a younger and more insecure designer. The character he created was so different and fun, and Antonio absolutely holds the screen when he is on. You can't keep your eyes off him. I would never have come up with those ideas on my own. Welcome, Huggy Bear.

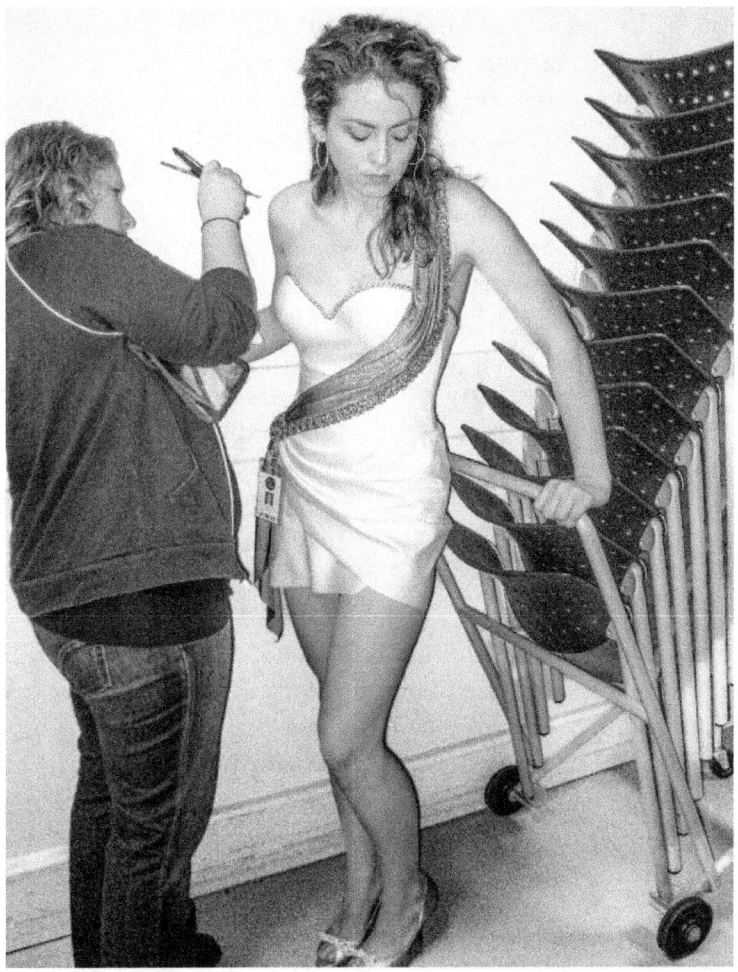

Anabella Casanova, one of the leads, getting touched up
by makeup artist Susanne Snell
Photo by Amber Thomson

Of course, working with the film students was one of the best parts of this experience too, and was the beginning (though I didn't know it at the time) of my years of teaching at UNLV. Few film students are forced by their parents to go into the arts. Those who do, *want* to be there and are passionate about it. Though *Stealing Las Vegas* was released in 2012, there are still alumni of the crew here in Vegas and in LA working in the film business, and crediting *Stealing Las Vegas* with inspiring them to believe that they could do it.

Teaching eventually evolved into an official contract as Part-time Instructor, so I've been teaching a new group of students what it means to be a costume designer two semesters a year. They learn to collaborate with the rest of the project's creative team, working with directors, actors, cinematographers and production designers on weekend shoots, which are then shown in class on our gorgeous state-of-the-art Dolby Amos screen, and where they receive critiques. One of the things I have tried to do as a very advanced-age professor is understand what twenty-year-old film students love, what they like to watch. At the beginning of each semester, I ask them all to name five of their favorite films. They don't know it at the time, but then I make a point of watching as many of those films as I can. I have slogged through lots of horror films, a film with themes of cannibalism, sci-fi films with heroes in rubber suits, and to my surprise, even Jim Carrey in *The Grinch Who Stole Christmas,* which I had never seen before.

I also tell the students that they may call me Diana in our private conversations, but in class, they are trained to call everyone with their proper title. I am "Professor Eden" or just "Professor" At first, it startled me a bit with its formality and respect, but I quite enjoy it now. Perhaps it elicits a touch of maternalism in me, as I almost hear it as "Mom" but with more respect and less baggage. How long will I continue to teach? At this point I don't know. I still love it, and love seeing my students blossom with a little encouragement. And when they tell me I have changed the course of their life, I just glow.

Sadly Professor Menendez died suddenly of heart failure in February 29th, 2024, leaving behind his wife of a few months, devastated students and bereft colleagues who all adored him.

Professor *Francisco Menendez and I at a UNLV celebration*

Another highlight of my early seventies was a job that made me feel very relevant and part of Las Vegas history. I got a call from a LA friend who had recommended me to George Stevens, a well-known producer. He produces all the Kennedy Center Honors galas, among other things, and was about to produce a very lavish star-studded gala, the opening-night concert for The Smith Center, the long-awaited theater complex in Las Vegas. He needed someone to costume his opening artist, trumpeter Arturo Sandoval, costume the band members and dancers, and make sure all of the stars had everything they needed for the big night, including Jennifer Hudson, Neil Patrick Harris, Carole King, Martina McBride, and heaps more. I could hardly wait to say yes! Production flew me to Los Angeles for a couple of hours to fit Arturo Sandoval. A young production assistant (he looked about sixteen to me) picked me up at Burbank

Airport and I felt really royally treated. We went to Arturo's house in the West Valley where there was a production meeting going on. Arturo was a little grumpy at first as I asked him to try on some shirts and a brown leather vest, but later I found him to be the sweetest.

Until 2013, Las Vegas had no place for legitimate theater and entertainment other than the headliner venues in the hotels or the Cirque du Soleil shows. Though *Phantom of the Opera*, *Mama Mia*, and *Jersey Boys* all had healthy runs in Las Vegas, they played in the major casinos in shortened versions so that the patrons could get back out to the blackjack tables. But in 2002, a group of financiers got together to plan and finance a new theater complex that would make Las Vegas proud and provide several stages for the best of American and international ballet, opera, and orchestral companies to perform, as well as a full Broadway season. Reynolds Hall in the Center would be a large European-style theater based on the great opera houses of Europe. Another smaller venue would be a cabaret with an intimate vibe and would showcase jazz, pop, and musical groups. It would also include a black box theater for experimental and lab performances. The Smith Center's design was inspired by the 1930s style of the Hoover Dam and has a sleek Art Deco look. They broke ground in 2009 and in March of 2012, it was ready to open.

I had the fun of exploring the inside of The Smith Center before it was open to the public, and got lost many times as I searched out hallways, boxes, and private rooms. What spacious and beautiful dressing rooms there were for the stars—not like the tiny spaces in the old theaters when I was touring! The Wardrobe Room was bare until I moved in, and the sewing machines and wardrobe racks arrived to make it a workable space. Two days before opening, my wardrobe crew was in place, and we fit the dancers. I had ordered six little black jersey dresses from Amazon, each one a little different, and then had the fun of having each one altered to fit and adding a little subtle bling. Yes, sometimes bling can be subtle!

The night of the gala was one of those special nights where everyone seemed to be in a good mood. Carole King floated around the backstage hallways, saying what a joy it was to be singing again. Violin practice notes could be heard coming from Joshua Bell's dressing room. Arturo had a bit of a panic and told me his wife had packed the wrong bow tie, and it wouldn't fit his neck, so Diana to the rescue.

I was just coming down the hall when I heard my name being called.

"Diana, come quickly, Laura's zipper is stuck, we can't get it up! She's on in five!"

Broadway star, Laura Osnes, was minutes from making her appearance on stage. I rushed over to see, and indeed it was caught at the waist in a mess of black tulle. "Oh no, she said, "I borrowed this dress and it is a designer vintage". What a pro! She stood still while I tugged and tugged, her cue getting closer and closer. "Get big safety pins ready," I barked to the dressers. Just in time, the errant zipper extricated itself and zipped up, and she was off to the wings to make her entrance.

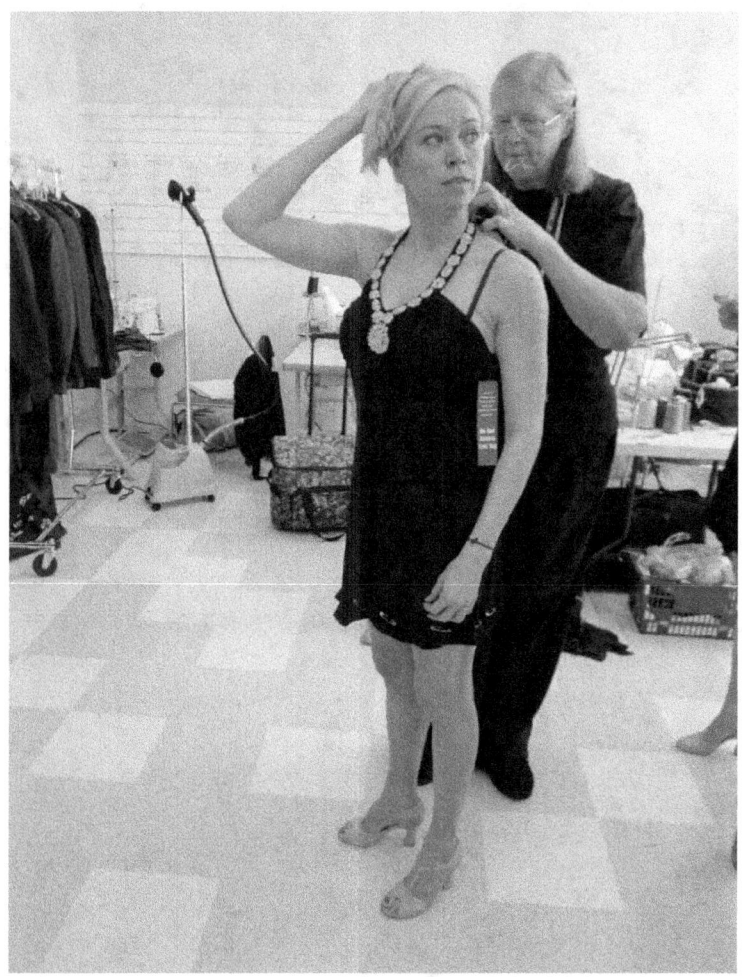

Brunie (Diane) Eichler, my wardrobe head,
fitting one of the dancers for the Opening Gala

Broadway star Laura Osnes arrives on the red carpet,
Neil Patrick Harris MC's the Gala

Even one of the three titans who built the Smith Center sent an SOS from the wings that he was in his tux, ready to make his entrance for his speech, and realized he had no cufflinks and studs. Once again, Diana to the rescue, as I always carry spares in my kit.

My position as costume coordinator for this momentous opening night concert was so gratifying. Ironically, the location was downtown overlooking the train tracks and the old train station I stopped at in 1961 when I was a young dancer on tour with *My Fair Lady*, a twenty-minute stopover I share in my first book. I'd come full circle after fifty-one years.

CHAPTER 4
Bulbous Buttocks and a Return to Theater

A couple of years into my pseudo-retirement, I was getting known around town (a bigger fish in a smaller pond, no doubt). One of my new contacts recommended me to a well-established Las Vegas resident of some means who produced the Opera Las Vegas. I was invited to costume their newest, full-scale production of *Don Giovanni*, featuring five singers and a conductor from the Metropolitan Opera of New York, and directed by Jonathan Loy, also from the Met. The rest of the cast were to be local singers.

Don Giovanni is actually set in 17th century Spain. However, director Jonathan envisioned a modern-day production of the opera with the principal characters dressed in shades of black, grey, and white, and the chorus (usually the "peasants") dressed as hipsters from the Brooklyn Heights section of New York, all in bright colors. Jonathan and I exchanged research images and got along famously. He told me, "I *love* what I'm seeing so far. You totally get what I am going for here." I was definitely new to opera. As I attended the first rehearsals, what struck me as hilarious was all these casually dressed men and women in shorts, T-shirts and flip flops transform the moment they started to sing. Their posture changed, and their voices emerged high fallutin' and, well, opera-like.

We had two weeks of rehearsals as I gathered costumes and did fittings, and then two complete dress rehearsals in Artemus Hamm Hall at UNLV. But all was not well. After the first dress rehearsal, the woman who hired me emailed that "the costumes on the supers (the young folks) were a little curious."

She continued, "Several people since my email exchange with Jonathan commented on the oversize fannies in skin-tight, bright-colored attire. I found myself fixating on bulbous buttocks and losing track of what I should be watching on the stage. I don't want big, pink derrieres to be what the audience remembers about Don G."

I wrote back, "The hipster look is a very contemporary look, and the bright colors are meant as a contrast to the black palette of the principals. I'm sorry not everyone likes it. It's an adjustment from the traditional look. I do understand that."

I was trained to answer to the director for all creative questions, so I next wrote to Jonathan, "Do I make *any* changes to satisfy the opera ladies? I have one dress that I can put on Judy, probably the widest pink derriere, but then again, should I leave well enough alone? "

His response? "We're not changing a thing :) Some people like ethnic butts, lol."

Needless to say, I was never asked back to design another opera.

But more theater? Yes.

The creation of the blue gingham Dorothy dress a few years ago had reawakened my love of sewing and reminded me just how much pleasure creating garments, especially pretty ones, brings me. In Los Angeles, my Bernina sewing machine had been relegated to the closet for so many years while I was designing professionally, and it only made an appearance when a personal hem was needed or some new pillows for the sofa. Besides, in LA I had no dedicated workspace, so the machine got hauled up onto the dining room table. There was a strong possibility that various threads and pins would land on the floor. Of course, everything had to be pristine and put away by dinner time.

With our new house in Las Vegas, I had an entire workroom (technically the third bedroom) upstairs for my sewing room, and I could just shut the door without worrying about the vision of a tornado-ravaged space disturbing the appearance of order in the house. The only area I sometimes had to take over was the kitchen, where the island provided the perfect height and width for my cutting board. It was here that Dominic was most territorial. I had to *promise* that every last vestige of my production was out of sight by the time he came home from grocery shopping and the kitchen was once again his domain.

One evening, Dominic was at work at "Tony' n Tina's Wedding" and I was on the sofa watching TV when an email came in, asking me if I was available to sew a red dress for an upcoming show. The producer sent me a sketch, and it seemed a fairly simple affair. He said he needed it *four* days from now and could he bring the actress/singer in question by for measurements as soon as possible, in fact, that same evening?

An hour later I opened to the door to a lovely brunette actress and the producer, Ethan Walker, a gorgeous young man, only twenty-eight, I was soon to find out. He was producing a live show on The Strip called "Piano Man" based on the music of Billy Joel, Elton John, and Barry Manilow. He offered to pay me *in advance* for my work, something which happens as often as ice forms on the equator.

Again, I was off and running. On completion of the red dress, Ethan asked, "Can you make another dress, this one in yellow, and can you have it finished next week?" Next week? Sure, I said.

Ethan and I got along like a house on fire. We went out for dinner one night and talked non-stop for three hours, much of which was about his venturing out as a fifteen-year-old from his home in Australia to join an Irish dance company in Belfast. He persuaded his parents to let him go and managed to secure a role in the company by lying about his age. One year later he joined Micheal Flatley's *Lord of the Dance*.

Anyway, despite the fifty years age disparity, I felt no awkwardness conversing with such a young person. Our early years as teenaged dancers showed remarkable similarities. That is the joy of the arts—age is no barrier. I felt a partnership being born.

Next thing I know, I've said yes to more costumes: two red lace mini dresses with red feathers at the hem (Ethan even came over and helped me glue on rhinestones), two purple mini dresses with fringe, and two more long satin gowns. I was sewing long hours, but on my own schedule and loving it.

The show itself was a joyous medley of songs I loved, with attractive performers performing non-stop for the ninety-minute run of the show. I could have watched it night after night.

Another client who came my way was Nina DiGregorio, a Las Vegas native and UNLV graduate in music. She was/is a rock violinist and arranger, as well as an astute businesswoman, and had formed a group called Bella Electric Strings which appeared on Season One of "America's Got Talent." (as Bella Rumore). The women played all around the US and were planning a show called Bella Disco Strings, based on the 1970s.

I first met them in the office of production designer Andy Walmsley who had designed American Idol and So You think You Can Dance for many years. All the violin performers were there too, all chiming in with their opinions for what the final look should be. Eventually I got to design five different over-the-top bellbottomed jumpsuits in silver and gold lame, bedecked in plenty of bling and feathers. It was right up my alley. Rhinestones and more rhinestones!

2 red lace dresses with feathers in work

"Piano Man" performers on stage
Photo courtesy of Ethan Walker

The Bella Electric Strings, all dolled up in bellbottom jumpsuits.
Photo courtesy of Nina DiGregorio

In a way, I was returning to my earliest days of costuming, where I did all the sewing, fitting, dyeing, and embellishing of the costumes myself. But this was different. I was feeling involved and creative, and *far* from being put out to pasture.

CHAPTER 5
AGE 73: Slowing Down While Still Trying to Keep Up

As the year rolled on and I turned 73, I still felt vibrant and healthy, but my physical stamina was deteriorating. Of course, I didn't want to admit it because that might take me out of the running for jobs and put me in that pasture where I didn't want to be. I have always liked a good eight hours of sleep, but now I found myself tiring more easily and having a harder time being on my feet during the long hours of film work. However, as the girl who can't say no, when my friend and fellow costume designer, Salvador Perez (and president of the Costume Designers Guild in Los Angeles), told me he was coming to Las Vegas for three weeks to film *Think Like a Man Too*, and was looking for costumers, I had to recommend myself (among others) .

But wouldn't you know it, production scheduled mostly all-night shoots. For those of you outside the film world, that means that your "day" starts at 11 p.m. and goes until 11 a.m., more or less. We were filming at Caesar's Palace, and naturally, the Caesars company did not want us to interrupt the gambling activity of their customers, nor in fact, impact any aspect of their guests' stay. So, we filmed when the pools, hallways, restaurants, and gambling areas were mostly empty. Dominic and I agreed that this would be a great time for him to go to Buffalo and spend a week or two with his mother and sister, leaving a quiet house for me to sleep when I could. My first day's call was at 1 a.m. I tried to go to bed around 5 p.m. to catch a few hours, but it wasn't easy to fall asleep, and when my alarm went off at 11:30 p.m., my body was drugged with sleep and didn't want to get up and go to work one bit.

As I arrived forty minutes after midnight in the parking lot they had assigned the crew, and walked the seven-minute walk to our trailers parked out in front of the hotel, I asked myself, "Diana, wtf? What on *earth* are you doing?" Why, you might ask, could I not just step down gracefully and pick up my knitting? I was still fighting the idea of being relegated to the sidelines, being marginalized, and having the younger ones take over. I was the purest kind of mascot for FOMO, the fear of missing out. Why couldn't I, at 73, be happy at home doing relatively little? Because I have a fear of that "relatively little." A day on my calendar with nothing marked down on it is a scary thing for me. I have had places to go, things to do, and a schedule all my life, and had not yet learned the art of "dolce far niente," the sweetness of doing nothing. I had not yet found in retirement a replacement for the benefits I got from work— connection to other people, fun, a sense of contributing to a larger whole, and a structure I found comforting. So what if the structure meant a reversed 9-to-5 workday?

I expect myself to be productive every day. I can no more read a book, watch a movie, or sit out on the patio during the middle of the day than do brain surgery or cook an apple pie from scratch. Perhaps on the weekend? Or on a Sunday, which is a day off... but a day off from what? When I text my sister almost daily, I ask her, "What did you do today?" I should rethink this and perhaps ask, "What did you experience today? What did you enjoy today?"

Well, wisdom and inner stillness hadn't reached me yet, so I continued on *Think Like a Man Too.* One day, we were scheduled to film at the Caesar's Palace swimming pools. We were to start on camera as soon as it was daylight but had to be out of the area by noon, so they gave us a four-a.m. call to get all the actors ready. We had a couple of hundred extras (background players) to romp in the pool that day. Each one had to be checked to ensure they were wearing an appropriate bathing suit for the scene—nothing with brand logos, no pure white, no prints that were too bright (to distract from the principal actors,) and so forth. And to comply with the PG rating they were hoping to get for the film for a wider release, they didn't want girls wearing really brief thongs, with most of their buttocks exposed. So, guess what job I was assigned (and at 5 a.m., too)? Once dressed, I had to ask each female background player to open her robe and show me her bikini, then turn around so I could assess how much derriere was showing. I was the Butt Police! (Dominic quipped that he would have gladly done the job!) I wondered what my parents would have thought... "We put her through college, sent her to Europe, and for this? Where did we go wrong?"

We were shooting in June, which is usually hot in Las Vegas, but apparently, we were experiencing "the hottest June on record." Outdoor scenes, even around a swimming pool, were brutal, and we could feel the heat rising from the cement. Set medics came around with washcloths soaked in ice water for us and made sure we were hydrated. Nevertheless, we were in 114 degrees for hours on end.

"How can you *live* here?" the out-of-towners asked with thinly veiled disdain. (They mainly consisted of the crew from Los Angeles who thought of their town as the rightful epicenter of film production anyway.) But we locals had to persuade them that we normally do *not* stay out in this heat for eight to ten hours a day, and that our summer is like other people's winter in that we stay mostly indoors. And we don't have to worry about shoveling snow or chipping ice off our windshields.

But my stamina was starting to be an issue, and I worked hard to conceal that from my team. No way I was going to leak that I wasn't up to the task and, that at seventy-three years old, I wasn't totally able to do what all the younger folks were doing. No one wants a whiner. I made good use of the time, though. I gathered lots of updated information on what professional set costumers do. I had been in the top position as a costume designer for a long time in Los Angeles, and, since I started my career in the early 80s, much more technology has been introduced and is now widely used. I needed to be in touch with the latest ways of doing things. I wanted to have the latest techniques, forms, and procedures so I could teach my students at UNLV and prepare them for their eventual career in the costume department of a film. I secretly photographed how the trailer was organized and snuck copies of continuity tags and work reports as material for future teaching.

Eventually, my time with *Think Like A Man Too* came to an end, and I was happy to hear the final "That's a wrap!" I received nice paychecks, accumulated some union benefits, and had a reasonably good time, other than at 3 a.m.

You would think I had learned my lesson about suitability at my age for film work. But three months later, I got a call about a four-day job on the film *Step Up All In*, part of the dance film series. Every instinct in my body said, "Don't do it."

"Are you crazy? asked Dominic. "I only just got you back from death's door!" But I quoted back to him from one of his favorite movies *The Godfather,* "Just when I thought I was out, they pull me back in!"

In truth, I was very lucky that Dominic was so supportive of pretty much whatever I wanted to do. I got to do what I loved, and he got unstructured time to pursue his interests without me looking over his shoulder. The only household chore he drew the line at was laundry. We always kissed before one of us set out for the day and we always asked,

"What time will you be home?" I knew whatever ungodly hour I got back there would be food in the fridge, and probably a good meal waiting for me.

This time, on "*Step Up All In*" it was not about the chance to learn or the paycheck but about the dancers. Some of the top contemporary dancers in the film, such as "Twitch" (Steven Boss) and "Comfort" (Fedoke), were dancers I had watched in the series *So You Think You Can Dance*. They were rock stars in my eyes. The job would also be night shoots (arghhhh), but only four nights. I thought, it's only four nights, I can do that. As it turns out, they had already filmed all the dance scenes in Vancouver, Canada, and were just coming here to film the Las Vegas location scenes. So, I would not get to see them dance.

The wonderful late Stephen Boss ("Twitch") and star Ryan Guzman pose for wardrobe continuity shots

A scene we filmed one night at the Las Vegas Neon Museum, a unique outdoor experience where all the iconic original marquees from the early Las Vegas casinos have been restored and put on display, turned out very special for me. It was cold that night, and I had been assigned to dress Briana Evigan, the female star. As we sat in her trailer waiting for her to be called to set, I mentioned that I had been a Broadway dancer, only to discover that Briana's mother had also been on Broadway at the same time. I thought we might even know each other. I love my connection to dancers, no matter what generation.

One unexpected connection I made was with the film's director, Trish Sie. As the director of a major feature, she was completely absorbed in directing the actors and completing the scenes on schedule. I was just one of the two hundred or so crew members working at the peripheries to make our departments run smoothly. She had no idea who I was. But as luck would have it, we both emerged from stalls in a public Ladies' Room at the same time and were washing our hands at the sink next to each other. I turned to her, identified myself, and gathered the courage to ask if she would be willing to come back to Las Vegas in the fall and speak to the Cinefemmes group at UNLV, a group of mostly women filmmakers. She agreed on the spot. My worlds of costuming films and teaching at UNLV now officially merged.

Getting a hug from Trish Sie after the UNLV/Cinefemmes event

On the film, I worked eighteen hours the first day, sixteen for the next two days, and the last day was another ungodly eighteen. We were in a nightclub at Planet Hollywood, and the filming went on and on. I was *so* ready for this to be over. Sometime around 3 a.m., there was to have been a scene outside with (I kid you not) a Roman gladiator guy, and the actor in question had not shown up. He was one of these people who dressed up in costumes and worked on the Strip, posing for pictures with tourists for tips. He was to be only in the background, and had no dialog, but when he didn't show up, the director was upset. She really wanted him. We got word that there had been a request that we somehow "come up with" a substitute gladiator costume. Really? At 3 a.m.? Costumers rarely say a firm no to a request, no matter what challenge is thrown at them, but when we got the word, we were still dumbfounded. I was so tired by this point that I couldn't even think how we would accomplish this request. I'd used up my second wind, my third wind, and all my adrenaline. The A.D. (assistant director) pulled an extra from the crowd who looked big and beefy enough to be the new gladiator. We asked housekeeping at the hotel if we could have a bed sheet. We tore it into a long strip the length of a man's pleated Roman-style skirt and then pressed the pleats with our iron. We made him Roman sandals by cutting up the covers of a three-ring binder for the soles and then using grey masking tape (gaffer's tape) to make loops. We found some thick string for the ties. We borrowed brown leather belts from a couple of the camera and lighting guys, sprayed them gold (thanks, art department), and made a belt and a cross-the-chest strap. The props department came up with a sword. We even took a tin foil bridal headpiece lying around, cut laurel leaves, and made a laurel wreath for him. Voila! I don't know how we did it, but we did. Not an Oscar-worthy costume, but it would do in the background.

I felt my brain had been turned inside out, and my body whipped and beaten—we now were at hour seventeen of our fourth day. And I was about to turn friggin' seventy- four! A garden and a knitting group were looking better by the minute.

But this was not to be my last. I was back to designing one more low-budget feature. This one was downright fun! It was a fantasy/horror film originally called "Drowned," later renamed "Lake Mead." The fun part was that we spent a week at Lake Havasu and two days on Lake Mead, cruising around the lake on boats as filming took place. Yes we had to roll our wardrobe racks over wooden docks and into the boats, which was a challenge, but then we got to relax on board most of the day! We also spent another three days in the abandoned mining town of Nelson, in the middle of the desert where the heat was brutal. Sitting under a little pup tent and putting wet rags around our necks didn't do nearly enough to keep us cool. But we had fun.

BEHIND THE SCENES FILMING "LAKE MEAD"

Me tea-dying something in the motel bathroom sink

Safety frogman protecting actors Emily Goldwyn and Fallon Goodson

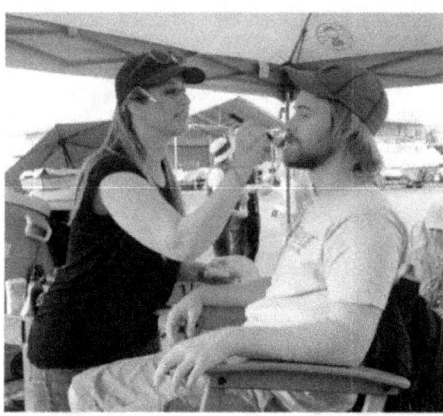

Makeup artist Debra Weite getting actor Christopher Meyers ready

Some behind the scenes filming "Lake Mead"
Photos by Amber Thomson

CHAPTER 6
TURNING SEVENTY-FIVE: The Trust

Turning seventy-five felt great! No regrets, no anxieties, no fear of death and other calamities.

Early in the year, I had a successful and fun experience as Las Vegas Costume Designer for a feature film called, "The Trust," starring Las Vegas resident, actor Nicolas Cage, and Elijah Wood, "Frodo" of *The Lord of the Rings* fame. The designer, Mona May, had already set the costume look for the two leads in Los Angeles, and I was to take over all the other characters once production started in Las Vegas. I had my favorite assistant, Amber Thomson, a new-to-me PA (production assistant) called Marta, and local costumers, all of whom I knew and trusted. We filmed all over Las Vegas, starting with the famed vintage lounge, The Peppermill, where I had frequently gone for brunch in the mid-70s during my days in town with Ann-Margret. We also filmed in The Riviera Hotel, on the monorail, at a bakery, at a machinists' shop, and out on a dusty road in the desert.

Some of the scenes were in seamier parts of town, since the story involved drug dealers and a heist, but as always when shooting on location, part of the adventure was showing up to each new location, never knowing what to expect.

One such scene was where women were making cocaine. We were told to park in a grassy area under a freeway overpass. My poor assistant, Marta, parked next to a truck which she thought belonged to the Props Department and in which she saw a very realistic looking dummy. Shortly after, we found out that the dummy was actually a real man, and he was dead! The police and coroner were called, and the area roped off, but it was a bit spooky, as we were coming and going near the area. The producers of course, were only worried that the police would shut down our filming and that we would get behind in our schedule.

Elijah Wood waits for his scene with Nic Cage to get going
Photo by Amber Thomson

For this same cocaine scene, I had asked the AD (Assistant Director) in a meeting about how to dress the background actors and had understood that there was nothing special here, just their regular casual clothes. *Wrong.* Not too familiar with cocaine making, I didn't know they had to be either naked or wearing something where they could not stash

44

some of the goods. The directors were flipping out. The scene was due to be shot in about half an hour.

"Hang on" I said, "I'll fix this. Just give me thirty minutes." I leapt into my car, drove past the decomposing man and the coroner, and headed to a medical shop that was right near us, across from the UMC hospital. I bought two packages of paper hospital gowns and raced back to set. Another disaster averted.

The role of Nic Cage's character's father was cast with Jerry Lewis, another Las Vegas resident, probably more because of his "marquee value" than to his suitability for the role. I called Jerry's assistant to discuss what type of wardrobe was needed to play a cop's aging father.

"This character is of limited financial means" I said, "just a simple working-class guy. The scene takes place in his kitchen so he should probably be wearing casual pants, perhaps khaki or cotton, a casual shirt, and possibly a well-worn cardigan. Nothing too bright. " Yes, Yes," said the assistant, "I totally understand. I am sure we can find a selection of Jerry's wardrobe that will suit the scene. I will make sure he brings a selection for you to choose from".

Nic Cage and Jerry Lewis deliver their scene, as seen on the monitor
Photo by Amber Thomson

On the day of filming, Jerry arrived with great fanfare, and surrounded himself with adoring bystanders to listen to his stories. But he was wearing a bright yellow silk shirt and navy blazer that he has worn on countless public appearances, and which was *totally* wrong for the character. He brought no other wardrobe and had obviously not planned to wear the character clothes. After many agitated conversations with the directors and producers, he was adamant about wearing what he arrived in. "It's comedy" he said brightly. We had to shrug and say, "oh well".

Me working on aging the heist coveralls for Nic and Elijah
Photo by Amber Thomson

A few days before the end of shooting, one of the actors in a minor part was giving me grief and complaining about the jacket I had chosen for him to wear. When I finally exited his dressing room, I said to Amber, "Can't he just shut up and put it on?".

"That's a great slogan," said Amber, "familiar thoughts for any costumer. Let's make t-shirts that say "JUST SHUT UP AND PUT IT ON".

And so we did, and our whole wardrobe crew wore them on the final day of the shoot. Everyone got the joke and laughed, and Elijah wanted one of his own.

Dominic had also been busy in the spring, loving making audiences laugh with his antics as the inebriated priest in *Tony n' Tina's Wedding* four or five nights a week. He would come home some nights quite giddy and like a mischievous boy, he would tell me how he climbed all over some old ladies who were laughing uncontrollably. He also landed some commercials and a small role on the TV series *Modern Family*, sharing the screen with Sofia Vergara. In addition, he booked hand-modeling jobs. Yes, he was an excellent hand model, a job he fell into in Los Angeles when working on *Star Trek Enterprise*. Production was looking for hands to stand in for Scott Bakula's hands in close-ups, twiddling the controls on the star ship. This is a very common occurrence in TV and films, so production can free up their star to get ready for the next scene. Dominic's hands won the job!

Then, one day, he was at Starbucks and, outgoing as he was, he struck up a conversation with a striking woman with long legs and accompanied by a dog with pink nail polish. She informed him that she had been a former leg model (think pantyhose ads) and now owned an agency called "Body Parts". She signed him up immediately and supervised a photo shoot where he featured his hands in various positions and holding various objects. He was a natural.

He continued to work from time to time as a hand model, and those fabulous fingers can be seen in a closeup driving a Mercedes, tenderly cradling a live tomato plant, and scooping out Blue Bunny Ice Cream. The night before he was to shoot a hand commercial, he would lather up his hands with a thick layer of Vaseline and hold up his arms in front of him like a surgeon getting into his operating attire. "Nurse!" he'd call out. I was to pull on his gloves. His hands emerged in the morning, soft as a baby's butt.

CHAPTER 7
MY SEVENTY-FIFTH BIRTHDAY:
The Second Honeymoon

My 75th birthday and our wedding anniversary on May 12th were celebrated in the South of France in Èze, a hilltop village between Nice and Monte Carlo. I didn't feel any older or have any life-changing revelations about the big silver event. I was healthy, Dominic was healthy, and we were still happy to be together. I was glad to use the occasion to celebrate the passage of time in a significant way, especially since it was also our 25th wedding anniversary.

"Let's recreate our honeymoon trip" suggested Dominic and I thought that sweet, and also a brilliant idea!

Our honeymoon's first night twenty-five years ago had been in Monaco in the Vista Palace Hotel, located on the Grande Corniche. From our balcony, we looked down upon the buildings of Monte Carlo. Windsurfers drifted down past our window as they made their six-minute flight from the cliff above us to a small beach way below.

From the hotel, it was a short drive to the village of Èze, which we immediately fell madly in love with. This ninth-century village is perched high atop the rocky cliffs and has spectacular views of Cap Ferrat and the magnificent coastline of the Côte d'Azur. Uneven cobblestones lead up through ancient arches into the tiny village and through narrow paths where climbing roses and brilliant bougainvillea flourish. At the top is the famed 400-year-old Chateau Eza, a five-star hotel and restaurant. It was a bit too elegant for us to afford a meal there back then, but we had a single drink in the bar to earn our right to snap photos off the balcony and promised ourselves that one day we would return.

Anniversary toast on the balcony of the Chateau Eza

Twenty-five years later, we did. We went for broke and booked three anniversary nights at Chateau Eza! Not a single thing seemed to have changed, though this time we were greeted like royalty. We were welcomed with lavender cocktails before being escorted to our room up some ancient stone stairs into the castle wing. Out our side window, we could see the Jardin Botanique Cactus Garden and the same magnificent view we remembered stretching out beyond it. We had arrived, seniors, old marrieds, but just as thrilled as newlyweds.

As per our usual way of traveling, we had rented a car. I thought a nice mid-size car would be just fine to get us from place to place, but Dominic, with his love of cars, pleaded with me "just once, can't I have the car I want?" So, I let him book it. Wouldn't you know he booked a BMW, ridiculously expensive and I had to do everything in my power not to protest. (*Shut up Diana, just go for it.*) From Eze, we drove (at some speed I might add) to a small town called Alba in the Piedmont region of Italy, famous for its annual truffle festival. This destination was also part of an unfolding story. Twenty-five years previous, I read in "Travel and Leisure" magazine about an up-and-coming new restaurant, the Osteria del Vicoletto, an emerging top-level establishment south of Milan. We had made it our mission to find this place. It was a two-and-a-half-hour drive from Èze through a segment of France, through Monaco, then north into Italy. We got a little lost but arrived at Osteria del Vicoletto at 2 p.m. only to find a big wooden door closed shut. Oh, no! We banged on the door. In a few minutes, a chef peered out, looking a little annoyed. I shoved the Travel and Leisure article into his hands and said in rather bad Italian, "We are on our honeymoon and have come to dine in your restaurant!" He had not seen the article and was excited to show it to his wife in the kitchen. We were ushered in and treated to the most divine three-course lunch, with wines for every course.

Perhaps we could return on our anniversary trip? Would it still be there? True to form, the restaurant was still there, same owner, same wife, and their "baby daughter." She had been in a crib when last we visited and was now an attractive young woman, managing the restaurant with Papa. Again, we were welcomed, given a fantastic meal, with many photographs taken and big smiles all around!

The family at Il Vicoletto welcomes us back after 25 years between visits

On our honeymoon, we drove from Alba north to Lake Como. Then, we never booked accommodation in advance but stopped when we felt like it. We arrived at the town of Cernobbio and checked into a reasonable-looking hotel right on the lake. There was a modest Harry's Bar in the square across from where we had dinner. That night, there was a huge storm, and we watched the rain and lightning from under the awning at the bar, laughing as we got a little wet and windblown. Twenty-five years later, we returned to Cernobbio, arriving in another rainstorm. I have a penchant for rooms with a view, and the place I found on VRBO was way up the mountain. The narrow winding road was not for the faint of heart, but the apartment was a charming two-story place with a view to die for, whether watching the storm over the lake or the brilliant sunshine a few hours later. "Is Harry's Bar still there?" we asked our host. Yes, it was, and yes, we did return for a meal. It had been enlarged quite a bit since we were there twenty-five years ago. We shared our story with our waiter, who brought us some after-dinner drinks, on the house.

From Lake Como, we took a side trip to Turin (Torino) where we had never visited, but which was home to two avid fans of the soap opera *Santa Barbara*, which I had costume designed in 1992. Pierpaolo D. had once contacted me for an interview, and we had stayed in touch ever since. Once again, show business creates connections all over the world.

And then to Venice, where we found an agreeable gondolier who was willing to find the same spot on the Grand Canal with the Rialto Bridge in the background to take our photo, matching it to our honeymoon gondola photo. Naturally, we brought the 25-year-old photo along with us. Dominic just adored Venice, as did I. One of the things about getting to be seventy-five is having these amazing memories and being able to look back on one's life with some measure of incredibility and amazement at how far we had come. I felt the most extraordinary gratitude for our life together and marveled how a twenty-six-year-old Italian-American rock musician and a forty-year-old Canadian-American costume designer could have transformed into this happy couple, still enjoying each other. "We really can't afford this," he'd sometimes say when we were on a trip. He thought travel was for the leisure class, not us working stiffs. But to me, this absence of work, striving, obligation, and the pure immersion in the senses of sight, sound, touch, is what a true vacation is, true joy.

"But Darling," I'd say, "we must have *more* of this. These moments of deserved indulgence, the good kind, the enjoyment in relaxation and happiness should no longer be considered rarified or unavailable to us." Luxury is not a price, it is a feeling, and we all deserve it.

Dominic at his happiest with a bowl of pasta and a glass of Barolo

I am so glad we threw financial caution to the wind and spent the money for the best. I'm so glad the cheap part of me relaxed enough to let Dominic have his BMW to drive around Italy. I don't regret a single overpriced bowl of pasta nor anything we bought that we didn't need.

I didn't know then that in five months he would be gone.

CHAPTER 8
Someone Has Collapsed

It was mid-November. I was a few miles from home, at a warehouse housing a production design company that built sets and signage for large events like festivals and concerts. I was sewing on some 12-foot-tall Christmas stockings, part of the holiday display soon to be mounted at the Bellagio Botanical Gardens. Four of these, each one different, would hang from the glass ceiling above the glittering, decorated Christmas trees. A friend designed the stockings and hired me to help with the sewing. I was making piping out of red and white candy cane fabric, wrapping it around a dollar-sized cord, when my cell phone rang. "Someone has collapsed in front of your house," the voice on the other end of the phone told me, "but we don't know for sure if it's your husband."

I didn't know how to react. The man who had called me, our community manager, told me he would call me back as soon as he knew something more. I still didn't know what to make of it, so I continued to sew, mindlessly.

Suddenly, a cold, hard thought crashed into my consciousness. What if it is Dominic? At this time of the morning, he usually runs his six miles around the neighborhood. Chills ran down my spine. I dropped the cheerful stocking and told my boss I was leaving. As I pulled up to our house, the street was empty, just one lone police car sitting at the curb. A police officer got out. "We're not sure who the man was," she said. "He had no ID on him, and the construction workers working nearby didn't know him. Can I come in?"

I let her into the house and immediately went to where Dominic's running shoes would have been. They were gone. "He's been taken to Centennial Hospital in an ambulance," she said, "and they are still working on him." We made the long, long journey across the north end of the valley on the I-215. The long journey, though, is really just twelve miles and normally takes about fifteen minutes. Today, it seemed like she was driving below the speed limit as if nothing in particular were happening. *"Can't she put on the damn siren,"* I thought, *"and fucking get there fast???"* She even tried to make polite small talk, as if we were two gals coming home from lunch at Mimi's Cafe. She kept reassuring me that "we don't know for sure who it is yet." But I knew, and I was very, very scared.

As we pulled up to the ER entrance, she sent me in ahead while she parked the car. *("Park the car? You're the fucking police, leave the damn car anywhere, for Christ's sake!")* I approached the reception desk, *(please don't start asking me for my name, social security number, insurance information, just GET ME TO HIM)*. They had been alerted. A lovely woman came out and started to take me back to "the quiet room". Something about her facial expression and body language told me the worst. "He didn't make it, did he?" She shook her head. No. "Come with me," she said, and so into "the quiet room" I went. A small grey room with no windows, a two-seater tweed sofa, and a side table on which sat a plastic plant and a box of tissues. Of course. It was not so much the quiet room as the where-you-stagger-to-a-seat-with-the-realization-that your-life-has-changed room; the tears-and-ugly-mucus-flying-from-every-pore-of-your-face room, the where you try-and-figure-out-who-to-call-first room .

I started immediately. I called my sister, who picked up right away. "Do you want me to come?" she asked. She was in Canada. "Yes," I said, and then I got off the phone. I couldn't put the news into polite words, I remember that. There was no preliminary "I have some rather bad news…" "I hate to have to tell you this, but…" I just remember being very blunt. I didn't have the energy or the inclination to be gentle.

Then I called Dominic's nephew, Christopher, who would have to relay the news to his mother, Dominic's sister, Donna. "Dom collapsed. I'm at the hospital. He died." Christopher took in a sharp breath and said nothing for what seemed like an eternity. Then he said, "This is going to kill my sister," and I knew he had a terrible task ahead of him. Again, I offered few details, as I myself knew so few of them. I got off the phone fast and then called Dominic's producer at *Tony and Tina's Wedding*. Got voicemail. Left a message, equally blunt. Helene called me back a few seconds later, sobbing. Dom was scheduled to work that night, and I knew she had to find an understudy to go on for him. The show must go on.

"Do you want to see him?" the counselor asked. I did, but I was scared. She guided me gently by the arm down the hall, past open cubicles with barely noticed ghosts in various stages of distress. Turning right into a room,

I first saw his ankles, wearing those missing running shoes, no longer white from running in Las Vegas reddish dust. Then his shin and calves, which hairless state had always amused me and made me slightly envious. And then the rest of him, lying there on a gurney, his orange running shorts the only brightness. A tube had been inserted into his side, attached by tape and bandages. Everything else in the room was steel grey or muted green, all cold hard surfaces and angles. Only the tubes, hooked in and out of machinery, had the suggestion of sinuous shapes.

His face was perfect. Still. Heavy. Those eyelashes that had first attracted me rested on his cheek. He looked exactly the same. No difference whatsoever other than his chest was not rising and falling with breath. So, is that it? Breath? Heartbeat? I didn't or couldn't understand the cellophane-slim difference between him being alive and not being alive. It was too overwhelming, as though my brain did not have the heart to engage these thoughts or try to understand. I just wanted to get away from that little room.

The counselor hovered behind me. I couldn't see or hear her, but I knew she was a few feet away. I was mute and confused. I wasn't sure even whether to touch him. I stood at his right side and moved around his head and kissed him quickly on his cheek. Was it his cheek? It felt foreign. There is a deep quietness, and stillness. The brutal mystery of death. It frightened me terribly. It was him, but he wasn't there. So heavy. So heavy. Suddenly, the concept of "dead" took on a meaning it had never had before.

I only stayed, perhaps a minute, maybe even less, I don't know, and then I asked the counselor to take me out. That was it. I couldn't stay one moment more. I couldn't take it. It was the last time I saw him, for about thirty seconds. Perhaps it was longer, it is hard for me to remember. I still wonder if I should have spent more time with him. Did he not deserve more than the brief minute I spent the room? Should I have touched him and told him how much I loved him? Was his spirit still in the room? Should I have lingered by his side and spoken to his spirit? What is a spirit? If it was hovering nearby, I certainly didn't feel it. All I saw was the stillness of a once-alive person, now not alive. I now knew what "a body" meant.

Soon, my friends, Bill and Ilene, arrived, having witnessed the ambulance at my house earlier and wondered what was happening. "Is everything OK?" they texted. Again, I was brutal. "No, I said. He's dead." They came right away.

Now, there was a whirlwind of questions from the hospital staff. "Do you want his clothes?" No, I didn't. Where did I want "the body" taken?

Dominic is now "the body." I had no idea about mortuaries, but Bill and Ilene suggested one that was not far from us, near the I-215, with a lovely view of the mountains. "Fine," I said. I think there were forms to sign. I don't remember. The ER doctor came in and said, "We tried everything, but there was nothing we could do." I had heard that before, so many times on TV shows. But being a doctor's daughter, I thanked him for his efforts. Bill and Ilene took me home, and another couple came over. There were more phone calls, including one from the organ donation foundation, apologizing for the call so soon after the loss, but decisions had to be made quickly. I said, "Of course, take everything you can." There were more questions about his health, but I was beyond talking, so Ilene took the phone. She said that whenever they asked a question she didn't know the answer to, she just made something up.

This decision by both Dominic and I to have "organ donor" on our driver's licenses was something we believed in. And it came as a great comfort some months later when I got a call saying that two people in the Middle East had received Dominic's corneas and could now see! I wished I had photos of them. And then, I also got a letter from someone saying her daughter had been in surgery and had received skin grafts from Dominic. But the best call was about six months later when I got another call from the foundation saying Dominic had produced many skin grafts. "What are they all used for?" I asked naively. "Mostly burn victims," she said, "and sometimes they are used in reconstructive surgery, such as after mastectomies." I started to laugh. I thought how truly delighted Dominic would be to know that he was bopping around on some woman's breast!

But on that evening, nothing was funny. I knew everything in my life would be different from now on. The finality of his death struck me to the core. Most things are not so irreversible, final, or uncontrollable. There one minute, gone, vanished, unseeable the next. Unreachable. Can't I have one more word? I have questions. I need to ask you about this.

That night, the most obvious of voids made themselves known. There was only one of us in the bed. The right side of the bed, so recently inhabited by a warm body, a husband, a cuddler, was now still and empty, the sheets cold but still showing the imprint of his body. Only our cat Sophia joined me on the bed, curling up near me. At least one extra heartbeat. Should be two. In the bathroom, his sink. The one on the right. His toothbrush. His shaving cream- - he shaved with an old-fashioned shaving cream brush and razor, still sitting on the edge of the bathtub.

The next morning, I went to make coffee, and there were his two favorite cups with his beloved Beatles on them. In the fridge, were all the ingredients he had just shopped for a mammoth "sauce," the pepperoni, the sausage, the fresh cloves of garlic, the meat for the meatballs—all waiting for him. Every corner, every counter, everywhere I looked was full of him. The following morning, my sister arrived. I remember her sitting on the edge of my bed as I came out of the bathroom. Suddenly, and totally taking me by surprise, came a wail from the very depth of my being which turned into a blood curdling scream. And then another. And another. They ended only when my physical energy could no longer produce them, my throat raw and my diaphragm exhausted from the muscular effort.

Some of my friends advised me to talk to his photo, suggesting it would bring me comfort. I tried. It made things worse. There he was in that lovely photo wearing the white straw fedora he bought in Italy, smiling out at me, looking so happy and pretty darned pleased with himself. But I can't bear to look at it. It makes me mad and just reinforces the reality that he is gone, the crushing reality so *irreversible* that I can't bear it. I just want to talk to him.

What would I say? I'd scream "You bastard! You are thirteen and a half years younger than me and *I* was supposed to die first. You reneged on our deal. You've left me, abandoned me. If I had died first, you would still be young and sexy enough to attract a new partner, but what the hell am I supposed to do? I'm seventy-five and heading downhill! How could you do this!"

CHAPTER 9
THE MORTUARY: The Un-Urn

It was a gray and gloomy day, cinematically appropriate for a trip to the mortuary. As I entered the address in the GPS, I realized to my horror that we were not going to the mortuary I expected. That one was on North Jones Street, where there were gorgeous mountain views and acres of green grass. Apparently, we were driving to the one on *South* Jones Street in a rather seedy part of town where there was not a blade of green to be seen. I felt badly because I thought I had wronged Dominic. He would want to be in a place suited to his upscale taste. I also felt badly for myself because I wanted to show my sister that Las Vegas was a really beautiful city, more than the gaudy strip of casinos that so epitomize Las Vegas.

Nevertheless, upon arrival at the mortuary, we were greeted by a lovely woman, impeccably dressed in a black skirt suit and white blouse. Her hair was combed back and slick with just a touch of grey. Even her nails were long and painted in a shiny dark vermillion. She ushered us down the hall and into her office. Our-lady-in-the-black-suit seated herself behind a beautifully polished and well-organized desk, and we took the two seats in front of her. She started to pull out the book to show me choices of urns for the ashes. I said no and plopped down in front of her a royal blue pottery jug with yellow lemons hand painted on it. Her composed face fell apart, mouth agape, and those perfectly plucked eyebrows raised. "It was what he wanted," I hastily added, a small white lie. I thought she might argue with me, but she could hardly argue with the late deceased client. "It has a chip in it "she said. "Yes, I know."

She couldn't know why this piece of pottery was so important to me, to us. On our trips to Italy, Dominic and I often bought small pottery items to bring back and to use for our Sunday pasta dinners. This one was purchased in the heart of Positano, and I particularly love this pattern, the deep blue background with the yellow lemons on it, so typical of the region. It would be perfect back home for The Sauce.

How do I explain to a non-Italian the importance of the Sunday dinners and "Sauce" in the cultural traditions of the Italian family? It is a marinara sauce made of canned or crushed tomatoes, tomato paste, breadcrumbs, garlic, and seasonings, with assorted meats. Everyone thinks *their* Mother's sauce is the best.

Every Sunday, without fail, in Italian households, "Sauce" is served with spaghetti, along with the same meatballs, the same pepperoni and sausage, and sometimes a veal chop for good luck. Never "A sauce" or "The sauce", just one word, "Sauce".

Dominic's life with waspy me in Nevada with no Italian family around made him miss this family tradition and so once in a while, he would say "Today I need to make 'Sauce'". Production started early in the morning with The Chopping of the Garlic, a mound so huge of the little pungent white bits I couldn't imagine any other flavor being tasted. But, oh, the house smelled divine. Then came The Making of the Meatballs. Dominic put all the ground beef and some veal in a large aluminum bowl with eggs and seasoning and then mashed it all together with his hands. He'd carefully scoop out portions of the mixture and form it into the most perfect little balls, then set them spaced like marching toy soldiers on a metal pan. "I just made 64 meatballs!" he would proudly announce to anyone listening.

Next came The Frying of The Meat. The meatballs would go into an iron pan full of the best extra virgin olive oil that money could buy. Then the pepperoni would be sliced and added. The sausage and the two veal chops, tied together with string with stuffing in the middle, were the last additions. And then the beloved "Sauce" would cook at a low heat for the rest of the day as all the flavors mixed and married, the aroma permeating the entire house. Dominic couldn't be happier than when in his kitchen. To one side of the preparation area sat a glass with a generous pouring of burgundy wine, sipped at certain intervals. As the glass emptied, Dominic's joy increased. Occasionally, he would burst into song, his own cover of the Puccini aria, "Nessun Dorma." Never was he happier than in this cooking ritual, a full day affair. When it was time to unveil his masterpiece and actually eat the meal, often just the two of us, all of the meat had to be scooped out and put in a separate dish. The spaghetti was put in a big pasta bowl with just enough sauce to cover it lightly. Then, the remaining sauce that was to be poured over each person's dish was served in this revered blue and yellow pitcher from Positano.

This is the pitcher that was planted in front of our-lady-in-the-black-suit. How much more fitting that his ashes go in this lovely royal blue pitcher to memorialize our wonderful Sundays together? Wouldn't his ashes be so much more comfortable in a jug that had contained the marinara sauce so many times, than in some imitation Greek urn? Anyway, once she recovered from this trauma, we moved onto the selection of container that his body would be put into before going into the fire. This was the first time I had ever been witness to or participant in these choices. At the top of the list was the simplest basic box and, of course, who would be cheap enough to choose that one? The second one had a satin lining and a pillow. "What on Earth does he need with a pillow?" I thought to myself. As a costume designer, I imagined better uses for this satin. So I was the cheapskate that chose the simplest box.

Next, I had to provide a recent photo of Dominic for the last stage of identification, and so I showed her one of his 8 x 10 headshots. She looked at it for a long time, scrunching her face up, a bit confused. "Good God," I thought, "they've got the wrong body. We *are* at the wrong place." But no, she said, "I think I know this man. I think I've seen him somewhere."

Lightbulb. "Have you ever seen *Tony and Tina's Wedding* at Planet Hollywood?" I questioned her. "He played the priest."

"Yes," she said, "I did. I remember him now, he was hilarious."

Oh, my God, Dominic so loved being recognized on the street by fans and now here he was, still recognized.

The last part of the saga was the delivery of the ashes to my house some days later. A time was scheduled for the delivery. A man arrived, looking uncomfortable in a suit that was too big for him. But he was nice enough and looked appropriately somber. I signed more papers that he brought in an emerald-green carry bag with the mortuary's emblem stamped on the outside. "Would you like to keep the bag?" he asked. I politely said "No, thank you," but was thinking, *"Good Lord, does he want me to advertise the mortuary as I go shopping at Trader Joes?"*

Dominic's ashes stayed in our house in the pitcher on the top shelf of my display cabinet. Ten months passed before I decided where to take him. A grave in the ground was not an option. He wanted his ashes scattered in Tuscany, another part of Italy we frequented. Apparently transporting ashes to another country is complicated with many hoops to jump through. I decided not to take the ashes to Tuscany.

There is nothing particularly Tuscan around Nevada, but there is the Colorado River, which is very peaceful. You can rent a pontoon boat and go downriver and hardly see anyone or anything other than the occasional kayaker, a few longhorn sheep, and some birds.

My sister had come back to Las Vegas with her husband to visit me, and I invited Bill and Ilene (who had been with me during that horrific day) and one other couple, Jim and Darleene, to join us. We rented the boat and puttered down the river for about half an hour until I looked at a little bay and said, "I think it's time." We hadn't prepared any ceremony, but Bill said a few kind words. My sister was tongue-tied and said nothing. Now my turn. Some of my anger poured out amidst a sudden torrent of tears, the anger of being left behind and how, being so much older than he, I was supposed to go first. Then our friend Jim's turn. "Well, I can't think of anything appropriate, and I hope you don't mind me saying this, but Dominic told me 'the sex was great.'"

A huge smile broke over my face.

And then I slipped him into the water.

CHAPTER 10
Did You Think Of Me?

Did you think of me as your heart stopped and you fell prone on the stones of our front walk? Did you think of promises broken? Did you not know that I would be bereft without you?

What did you see? Did you see my blue eyes pleading with you to stay a little longer? Or did you just see a flash of cement, your eyes closing as you fell?

Did you hear anything?
Did you hear the sound of my screams even though I knew not yet that you were fallen?

Did you think of us?
Did you think of us racing from the Jacuzzi to the bedroom at full speed to make wild passionate love? Did you think of us, sitting together under the olive trees in Tuscany, drinking red wine and thinking how lucky we were? Did you think of us going hand-in-hand to the movies every Sunday?

What did you feel? Rage? Surprise? Sorrow at leaving me behind so unexpectedly, for not staying around to take care of me and to make me laugh?

Did you think of me at all? I hope and pray that as you fell those few feet to the ground that every fiber of your still-working brain resounded with my image and that my love for you pulsed through your heart as it beat its final stroke.

CHAPTER 11
BACK TO WORK: I Can Do This

One week after Dominic's death, I went back to work. I'd been hired earlier in the fall for the movie *Jason Bourne*, one of the biggest movies to be filmed in Las Vegas in a long time. It was the latest and perhaps final installment of the blockbuster series starring Matt Damon, Tommy Lee Jones, and Alicia Vikander, fresh off her Oscar nomination for *The Danish Girl*. In fact, the six weeks that the company would spend in Las Vegas was at the end of a long shooting schedule that started overseas in Tenerife (substituting for Athens), London, Berlin, then Washington D.C, and now here in my hometown.

After my exhaustive four days on the movie *Step Up All In* the previous year, I thought I would not take any more film jobs with fourteen-hour workdays. I knew that at seventy-five years old, those jobs were really out of the question, ridiculous for senior-citizen me to attempt. But I still had serious FOMO, and the fact that Oscar-winning costume designer Mark Bridges was the designer for this project made me long to be involved. When I got his assistant's email in early November asking for recommendations for local costumers I knew I was hooked. No way was I going to pass up this opportunity, seventy-five years old or not. I was offered the position of costume shopper for Mark, a job I thought would be perfect for me. I knew the vendors in Las Vegas well, and I would be working independently and without set hours, *and* I'd be assisting this A-list Hollywood designer.

Then Dominic died.

I was terrified someone in the costume department would learn of his death and assume I would not be up to the job, so I sent an email assuring them I was ready and able to do the work and would keep any personal issues under wraps. I was frightened of being left behind, being left at home alone to mourn. Of course, I was putting off the inevitable

67

grief, which would hit me harder than I could ever imagine a few months later.

A week after Dom's death, I received the call with my start date for Monday and the location of the production office. I was excited to meet my new teammates, see the production area, and start doing what I loved to do. I remember driving down the I-15 on the way to work that first day and actually feeling good. I remember thinking, "This isn't so bad. I can do this. I am not crying 24/7 - I can do this." It was a bizarre kind of euphoria.

I greeted fellow costume team members in my new workspace. None of the out-of-town people knew about my situation, and I did not reveal it until my last day. But my local friends knew what had happened and would give me a hug and ask, "Are you doing OK?' as they searched my eyes for signs of my true feelings.

I set up my office space, installing the computer, purchasing the right supplies, and making my little area feel like my office home. And there was lots going on to intrigue me. Every day, massive cartons arrived from Europe, filled with dozens of costumes used overseas to be used again, mainly for the extras. Other cartons arrived with the principals' clothing, all immaculately labeled and encased in zippered plastic garment bags. Then dozens of wardrobe racks arrived, racks on which soon would be hung more costumes for the film's large cast. The spacious area assigned to the costume department suddenly became much more crowded.

There, I was okay. I was distracted, engaged, and around lots of people. But at night when I got home? I crashed. During the day I maintained the outer manifestation of me getting up, brushing my teeth, driving to work, interacting with people, driving around the town in my car, and spending lots of money from the film's large budget. Underneath the surface, the grief churned, my soul wailing and gasping for air. I refused to let the monster surface or break through my magnificent façade at work. What a battle! No wonder every fiber of my being was exhausted at the end of the day by the war between my inner and outer selves. And every night, exhaustion finally won. The next day, the battle began anew amidst the glamorous frenzy of work.

What does a costume shopper do? My job was to purchase hundreds of pieces of clothing, much of it for the background actors cast in many of the up-coming scenes. I was to shop for all the day-to-day requirements for the smaller roles, the stunt doubles, and anything else needed for the Las Vegas scenes. Only the stars' costumes were already established. First, I went to Savers, one of the large thrift shop chains in Las Vegas. I'd walk the aisles selecting countless men's and women's shirts in the required palette. When everything was piled so high that the shopping cart was about to topple over, I would head to the cash register, where I was greeted with curiosity and awe, as at least a hundred items were removed from their hangers and were ready to be put in plastic bags. If I happened to be there on a Tuesday, Senior's Day, I received the fifty percent discount. Here was one project where the budget was *not* a problem. The film's budget was a whopping 210 million dollars. And yet, I accepted the discount with gratitude.

Mark Bridges, the costume designer, arrived a few days later, bringing a fresh momentum. We went shopping together and shared a few laughs. He had no idea of my situation. Tall, elegant, and beautifully dressed, he moved up and down the aisles of the thrift store, exclaiming with glee when he found a treasure. It was hilarious to me. "Oscar-winner shops at Savers." I could see the banner headlines now.

One of the reasons the production had come to Las Vegas was that the final car chase sequence would take place down the Las Vegas Strip and be one for the ages. For the first time ever, Las Vegas Boulevard would be shut down for three nights to allow for the stunts and car crashes. The action sequence involved around two hundred vehicles, one hundred-seventy of which were destroyed. Car costs alone were close to half a million. The Riviera Hotel, recently shuttered for good, allowed one of the SWAT trucks to crash through its front door -- a one-time shot, so they had to get it right the first time. Back in the production office, I found it fascinating to hear the stunt guys discuss how they would make all the action sequences work for this specular series of crashes. They had a large table set up with a mock-up of Las Vegas Boulevard and miniature cars on it to plot the moves.

"Steve, you come down the center and on the count of five, Mack, you swerve across his front end, and Larry, on the count of two, accelerate and crash into him from the rear." I was desperate to photograph all these world-class stunt guys playing with their little cars, but it was strictly forbidden. We had all signed major NDA (non-disclosure) contracts, and nothing was allowed to get out.

After two weeks, production closed down to allow the crew to enjoy the Christmas holidays. I had promised Dominic's family I would fulfill our original plans to visit them in Buffalo for the holidays. We would hold a memorial for Dominic while I was there.

Even the dummies for the car chase "bystanders" needed wardrobe

I crashed right back into post-trauma feelings, right back into the reality of what had happened, with nothing to distract me. In Buffalo, at my in-laws' house, the fact of his death was everywhere. His sister's grief filled every corner, and I was on the edge of a complete meltdown most of the time. It was a ghastly two weeks, not due to anything the family did -- they were wonderful-- but some days I couldn't get out of bed, couldn't face more Italian cousins, more questions, and more holiday dinners. I was exhausted.

On my return to Las Vegas, I had one more river to cross and that was Dominic's Celebration of Life for his friends here. His producers at *Tony n' Tina's Wedding* had generously offered not only the Tony n' Tina theater, but to host the event and provide food and drinks. As the regular show went on in the theater that night, the event could not start until after the show was over and the audience gone at the late hour of 10 p.m. Dominic's heartbroken cast-mates had planned and rehearsed a medley of Beatles songs, and another actress performed a song I requested called "Put a Candle in the Window." Close friends gave heart-wrenching tributes honoring his remarkable spirit, delicious humor, and incomparable kindness. His closest friend Paul from LA, a professional musician and fellow Buffalo ex-patriot, was unable to get there, so he sent a poignant video of himself playing guitar and singing the Bob Dylan song "It's All Right." I put together a slide show of photos of him, from his baby photos through when I first met him, to recent photos. I planned something brief to say and re-wrote the lyrics to a classic Sondheim song from the Broadway show "Follies." I sang, and half spoke these lyrics:

Good times and bad times,
I've seen them all, and, my dear,
I'm still here.
Barolo and pasta sometimes,
Sometimes, just pizza and beer,
But I'm here.
I've stuffed my feelings
In my shoes.
Screamed a little,
Sung the blues,
Seen my beloved disappear,
But I'm here.
I've been through Broadway,
Sitcoms and red-carpet affairs,
Now I'm here.
Bellbottoms, minis,
jumpsuits and really big hair,
And I'm here.
I got through the rain with Diana Ross,
The MGM fire
Who's The Boss
But Dom came along
And changed my life; that is clear
I'll survive this loss,
because he was here.
Good times and sad times,
I've seen 'em all, and, my dear,
I'm still here.
Martinis with olives, sometimes.
Sometimes, just peanuts and beer,
But I'm here.

I've run the gamut.
A to Z.
Three cheers and dammit,
C'est la vie.
I'll get through it all because of you
And I'm here.

That was a Sunday night. Monday, January 4th, I returned to work on *Jason Bourne*.

CHAPTER 12
The Long Winter of Spring

I don't know exactly how it was decided, but our young friend Olivia came to stay with me for the first two weeks in January. I was blessed with having her take care of me in the most loving way. I met her through Dominic when she was an actor performing in *Tony n' Tina's Wedding* and we bonded immediately over the fact that she played a role I had originated, that of the Beer Stein Showgirl in the original film of *The Producers*. She reminded me that she was not a guest to be entertained but was there to hold space for me to do whatever I needed. During the day, when I was working, she argued with AT&T about closing Dominic's account, took his car back to the dealership for re-sale, and sent the death certificate to the vendors requesting it to close accounts. She also prepared meals for me. She recalls that I would come home and appear fine and then, seemingly at random, would start to get upset, like a quick thought of Dominic cracked the very delicate layer of normalcy I was attempting to maintain.

She also has a very poignant memory of me that in no way coincides with my memory. She says, "I have this vivid memory of your nightgown and robe. They were lovely. And the robe would catch the air and float behind you as you'd walk away. You reminded me of royalty. Your hair was done, your make up was on, but your eyes were pained."

Back at work, Olivia gone, still exhausted, every day seemed fifty hours long. I pushed through but my body wasn't holding up well. We were filming at the Aria Hotel, and the trek from my car in the parking lot to my office felt like ten miles of gravel. My legs felt like Jello. I would make it to lunch hour and wonder if I could make it to the end of the day. I'd make it to Wednesday and wonder if I could hang on until Friday. I don't even remember the weekends. I think I never got out of bed the entire time of those weekends, but I'm not sure.

During the week, there was still some fun to be had within the job, and daily crises to deal with. One day, I got a text from the costume supervisor saying that they could not find a pair of lace-up dress shoes for an actor playing a CIA agent. He wore a size 13 and *was due to film in 30 minutes.* Do you know how hard it is to find a size 13 classic dress shoe, lace-up, black, and get it to the wardrobe trailer on location all in thirty minutes? But I did it.

Another time I got an SOS they could not locate a black designer purse that Alicia Vikander had carried in a previous scene, and that would be needed for a match the next morning. "Find something of top quality," Mark told me as I headed to the luxury businesses at Crystals, the super high-end shopping mall next door to the Aria Hotel. As I entered stores such as Armani, Gucci, Burberry, Chanel, Dior, and others and mentioned: "Jason Bourne" (everyone in town knew about the movie), salespeople leapt to my aid, bringing me glasses of champagne and offering to put these $3500 purses on hold. I didn't need to fear that the modest little outfit I was wearing, and the lack of abundant gold jewelry made me appear an unlikely customer. I remembered the famous scene in *Pretty Woman* where Julia Roberts was shunned in a Beverly Hills shops until Richard Gere showed up to set them straight. Now, these salespeople were eager to pose with the selected purse so I could send photos to the designer. I started to feel guilty after the third shop as people had fallen all over themselves for me, and I didn't know which, if any, of the purses would be chosen. In the end, none were. Mark found something entirely different that evening that he was happy with.

At the other end of the spectrum, the 5 a.m. visits to Walmart to stock up on t-shirts for background actors playing kitchen workers were not much fun, and visits to Payless (alas, no more) to buy clogs and sneakers for the same characters even less so. Everything was a rush, so I was often on some kind of adrenaline high as I raced about town trying to save the day. Diana, Costume Shopper Extraordinaire, to the rescue!

As the weeks went on, the exhaustion I felt—bone-weary, soul-weary, to the edge of complete physical failure, possessed me. I still have dreams about it. And then I got even sicker. By now, it was late-January, a cold and sometimes rainy month in Las Vegas, and the European crew, who had already been working for eight months, were getting sick, too. One day, I called my doctor for some relief, but he said he would not prescribe antibiotics unless he saw me in person. He would stay late at the office if I could come after work. I drove myself clear across town in the wintertime dark and then sat in the exam room for an hour alone. When he finally came in and said, "What seems to be the problem?" I lost it. Maybe he didn't use those exact words, but that's how it felt. Apparently, I was on the verge of pneumonia, and if it got worse, I had to go to the hospital. He sent me home with my prescription, and I blubbered all the way back to the pharmacy, a mess of mucus and self-pity, alone in my car on the dark streets. The pharmacist told me I'd have to wait in my car for thirty minutes more while they filled it, and I sobbed some more as I sat in the parking lot. This was before I knew I could call a friend and ask them to help me or pick up my prescription. I didn't know I could have friends I could call for help. I had not allowed myself those friends before, as I always had Dominic. I learned better later. But this night, I was on my own, and it felt like the worst night I could remember.

When I finally got home, I fell into bed and wondered if I had the strength to ever get up again. But I did. I struggled to work a few more weeks, but by mid-February, things were winding down, and the production was getting to the end of its stay in Las Vegas. Matt Damon had finished his scenes and headed back to his home in Manhattan, while Tommy Lee Jones had already left for LA. There were some pick up shots left, and then we had to wrap up the production office, inventory the wardrobe purchases for the accounting department, and pack and ship things back to production's HQ. Mark saw me coughing and gasping for breath one day and told me to go home and stay home. Only then did I tell him about losing Dominic. His only reaction was stunned silence and then a soft "wow."

Finally, home and no longer employed, the real mourning began. I wore a fuzzy grey robe most of the time. The bed was strewn with the detritus of the despairing, odd bits of discarded clothing, cat hair, half-used tissues like white caps on a turbulent sea. I didn't shower, even finding comfort in the musky odor of my sweat and tears. A few friends came by, but I discouraged them with a note on the door saying, "Sleeping, please do not ring the bell."

I remember a few visits from friends and neighbors, but only a few. Was this as it actually happened or just as I remember it? I did not have close friends yet in the neighborhood. Did my family call regularly? Did anyone check on me to make sure I was still alive? I don't think so, but I could be wrong. There is reality, and there is the way I remember it, which was that I was alone day after day as I struggled to regain my health… and grieve. I received many kind notes in the mail (and many on Facebook). There was that period when Dominic was lauded as the most wonderful, kind, loving, and brilliant man that had ever lived, and our marriage was touted as an ideal love story. "When I saw you last at the screening," my film professor told me, "I commented to someone that you two looked so happy together, so perfect for each other." Our love story took on mythic proportions, the story of a 26-year-old young man who had won over an older woman and their glorious years spent together, traveling the world. It was the Facebook version, everything perfect. All the wrinkles Photoshopped out.

Some months later, at the Jason Bourne premiere

But then there were my dreams. Oh my god, the dreams! I have always been a good sleeper in the sense that my eyes remain shut for a good eight hours, and I am unconscious most of that time. But during those hours, my subconscious tortured me with dreams that left me demolished when I woke up. Dreams that Dominic wanted to leave me, leave our marriage. Dreams that he was moving out. Dreams that I was looking for a place to live. Dreams that we were dividing up our possessions. Dreams that I was pleading with him not to leave me. Dreams that I was trying to remember his cell phone number but couldn't, or that he wouldn't answer.

What was I to think? That he *chose* to leave me. I would wake with the debilitating conclusion that I was, at the heart of it, unlovable. I remained in that state of feeling unlovable for a long time. It was sometime in April before I peeked my head out of the cave.

One of the first things I did was to adopt a new cat, a cat about three years old who needed a new home. I already had lost Gina, one of the two sister cats Dominic and I had adopted as kittens, but I still had Sophia.

Here is Sophia's account of how things went down:

I was suffering, too. I was feeling the effects of my age—almost nineteen—and was a bit frail myself. It got harder to jump up on the bed, but I managed somehow. I missed Dad so much, and I felt so helpless regarding Mum's grief. I think I was losing weight, too, and my fur was losing its former sheen. Looking in the mirror, I could tell, "Yes, Sophia, you are one old cat."

But I had to hang on for Mum. She had lost Gina and Dad within three months, and I knew she would never survive losing me, too. So I had to hang on. I wasn't sure how long I could do it, but I knew I had no choice. Mum and I both hobbled along, doing the best we could. "How long can I last?" I wondered.

Sometime in the spring, a friend of Mum's called Amber came over, holding, of all things, a member of my tribe, a calico cat called "Nala." Well! What the hell! Feline fuck! Who was this, and how long was she staying? Am I to be replaced? Am I to have a new step-sister I never asked for and didn't know if I would even like? Who would get to sleep with Mum on the sofa and, even more importantly, on the bed?

Mum put up a partition in the living room, a dog barrier gate thing, to keep us from scratching each other's eyes out. But during the night, Nala and I had a talk.

"Listen," I said, "I am the top cat here, and I have looked after Mum all these months, and believe me, it hasn't been easy."

"I know," said Nala, "I heard what happened, and I am not here to replace you. My human just thinks that you may be tired and want to go to the Rainbow Bridge soon, and your Mum may need someone else to help her."

"Dammit, I am pretty tired and frail. Will you take care of Mum if I go? And be good to her, let her nuzzle you, and sleep with her?"

"Yes," said Nala, "I will do that."

"She likes it when you come upstairs and curl up next to her sewing machine and help her sew," I said." Do you understand?

"Absolutely," Nala said. "I love threads and pins. They are fun to push onto the floor."

"Will you meow loudly at 6:30 a.m. and lick her face, but then lie at her feet until she is ready to get up?"

"Yes," said Nala, "I promise."

"Will you carry on in the morning like you haven't eaten in a month and then turn your nose up at the food she puts down?"

"Of course," said Nala, "I am a cat."

I thought about it a bit and decided maybe it was time to quit, to let go. Mum was good to me, but it's time for the young'un to take over. I think I will go over here and lie down for a bit.

Sleep. Aaah, sleep. One last exhale. Nala, it's your turn. Be good to her.

CHAPTER 13
HALF A COUPLE: Feels Like No One at All

My challenge--to create a new version of me that could exist in a life without him. The great challenge of widowhood. After the loss, you have to find a new identity. For so long, it had been "Dom and Diana," "Diana and Dom." And then there was one. Gloria Lintermans, my former writing partner and friend, called the feeling "when half of two feels like zero." How true this is. How can half of Dom-and-Diana ever amount to anything? How can I have a social life, a travel life, or any life without the other half?

Dominic and I in Castelmuzio, Tuscany in happier days

You don't realize it at the time, but you have an identity as a couple. Here we had been the perfect couple, people said. We had a lovely house together. Dominic cooked, and I and worked in costumes. We spent every Sunday together at the movies. We traveled. We had a social life. We complemented each other in every way, like those carved wood face profiles that fit into each other. I took care of the bills, the organizing, the planning of travel and social events, the writing of thank you notes when required, and, oh, yes, the laundry. Dominic drew the line at the laundry. He took care of grocery shopping, organizing the kitchen, cooking *and* cleaning up (he didn't like the way I did it), being the charming host or guest, and keeping everyone fed and laughing. It worked so well! Even our look as a couple worked. Dom was a few inches taller than me, with dark hair and eyes next to my red hair and blue eyes, his extroversion next to my quieter aura.

Our friends knew that perhaps I was the quiet strength behind the throne, as it were, but Dominic was the fun one. He was the one who lit up a room when he entered it. He was the one who made you feel at home and relaxed the moment you crossed our threshold. Dominic and I were undoubtedly an unusual couple, coming from such different backgrounds and with a thirteen-and-half-years age difference. However, we had some similarities at the core—we both struck out at a very early age from the comfort of our homes and families to seek fame and fortune. And though neither fame nor fortune rained down upon us, here we were all these years later, successfully doing what we loved.

When we first planned the building of our last house, the house that would be our retirement home in Las Vegas, we made a deal. He would have total control of the kitchen design (I had no problem with that) and I would have total control of the swimming pool and backyard. Not to say he didn't have annoying opinions, about what trees should be planted and what shape the pool should be, but in the end, it was my choice.

You spend a lot of time in a marriage working out the tacit agreements, and at first, you probably go by what is the norm. But the longer you are together, you discover what each person is good at, and claim those areas as your own. Over twenty-five years together, we figured out who did what and how we fit together. These tacit agreements weren't in place at the beginning of our relationship. I made an effort to be the meal provider initially, thinking that was sort of my duty as a good girlfriend, even though, if you'd asked me at the time, I would have vehemently insisted I paid no mind to traditional roles. But I did try. I could make steak and one chicken dish from the " I Hate to Cook Cookbook." Soon, Dominic offered to make his family's classic pasta and Sauce for dinner, which I gladly accepted.

I continued doing the basic weekly shopping by slipping a wishlist and a blank check under the locked door of our small local grocery store on my way to work at six a.m. and asking them to deliver it when they opened. No lingering in the aisles and squeezing the mangoes for me, thank you. After I screwed up buying the right ingredients for him enough times, Dominic took over more and more of those chores. (Who knew olive oil wasn't the same as extra virgin olive oil? And how can you be "extra virgin"?)

Also, our traditional male/female roles were somewhat reversed in other areas. I was working full-time as a costume designer, and he was freelancing as a musician, an airline employee for a period, and then an actor, so it made sense that he took care of the house. My challenge in the months after his death was to reinvent myself, to create a new version of myself that could exist in a life without him. I had to learn all over again how to grocery shop, make and entertain friends, and be happy. Some of these skills took time and much work to acquire.

With Diana- and- Dominic no more, I was adjusting to living alone for the first time in thirty-five years.

It was not all bad. I could fart with impunity, and I could load the dishwasher any damn way I wanted.

So, where to start with this new life as only Diana?

CHAPTER 14
EMPTYING THE CLOSET: Goodbye to Big Blue

One of the hardest chores (as if there were easy ones) was deciding when to get rid of Dominic's clothes. Friends advised me not to rush it, to do it whenever I felt up to it. Even the words "get rid of" felt harsh and dismissive, like I was tossing him out.

I was still working on the movie, *Jason Bourne,* when I first re-purposed some of his shirts. In my job as shopper for the film, I was purchasing hundreds of shirts every day for the movie's background actors and realized that many of Dominic's shirts were in the perfect palette for the film-- olive green, muted blue, soft taupe. I gathered up at least a dozen and snuck them into the wardrobe room and onto the racks, somehow feeling that explaining where they came from would be awkward, if not slightly creepy. But I knew Dominic would love "being in the film." I even saw designer Mark Bridges stop and look at one of them as if admiring it, and it made me smile.

I had always raided Dominic's closet for theater and film projects, with his permission, of course. Most of his ties were fair game, and who else did I know who had cufflinks, tie bars, or even a pearl stick pin (all of which I used to impress Eric Roberts in the film *Stealing Las Vegas*)? Only one time had this practice ever been a disaster. I borrowed a favorite well-worn red t-shirt he'd been gifted by his cousin to demonstrate to a class of high school students the art of aging a t-shirt. I wanted to demonstrate how hundreds of washings and wearings could fade and soften a t-shirt, perhaps stretch out the neckline a little, until it looked like this beloved sample of Dominic's. However, unbeknownst to me the t-shirt got into the wrong pile and was transformed by an ever-so-eager student into a zombie t-shirt, complete with rips, tears, and blood stains. I had to return home empty-handed and shame faced. His reaction wasn't good. I thought my days of raiding his closet might be over forever.

Getting rid of the physical possessions of someone you love is like losing the person all over again. I wanted his clothes left hanging in the closet, reassuring me that he would return and wear them again. I ran my fingers down the sleeves of those shirts and jackets and inhaled his smell. I touched those rakish straw Borsalino hats, as I remembered him buying them in Italy and wearing on our trips. So many items were so emotionally charged with memories, I often started to sort and then could go no further. How he loved his clothes. How rare to find a man that so adored buying and wearing good quality clothes, and how unusual to find a man who wore jeans and a sport coat to the movies when most people would just throw on sweats and a windbreaker. One guy at the local movie theater even called him out on this, saying, "Hey dude, aren't you a little overdressed?"

I was loathe to give his suits to Goodwill, as I felt the shoppers there would not appreciate the quality of what they were looking at. I couldn't bear the thought of them flopping around on a wire hanger (God forbid!), squished between other half-shredded cast-off items, perhaps even falling on the floor. It wasn't that Dominic had a huge budget for top-of-the-line clothes, but we did have the help of friends in the menswear business (Sy Devore, Tommy Bahama) who enabled him to get deep discounts. I held back on those suits for a long time until I eventually had a friend take them to a veterans' center. Honoring the veterans was the least I could do.

He loved his Tommy Bahama collectible shirts with the designs on the back. One of his favorites was black rayon, short-sleeved with a martini motif. He loved his martinis! I always made one for him the moment he returned from performing at night in *Tony n'Tina's Wedding*.

Two sport coats in particular were hard to give up. One he called "Big Pink". We were in Rome many years ago and stopped by a discount menswear store we had discovered by chance. There, he saw a pink silk sports coat! It was a dusty coral pink, three button, single vent, lined with a pale salmon fabric with narrow grey stripes. He fell in love with it. With his dark eyes and hair, he looked dashing in it, especially when he paired it with black dress pants and a black polo shirt. Real men definitely wear pink, and it suited him so well. Even though silk, the jacket seemed to make it through endless cleanings and took on a life of its own. Big Pink was seen on Dominic at all the major events of our life together. It's in all of our 25th wedding anniversary trip photos. I couldn't give it up. It still hangs in my closet.

Dominic sporting his new favorite, "Big Pink," in Rome, 1999

The other favorite was Big Blue. He spotted the sportscoat in a Versace window when we were in Venice, and at the time, in my typical Diana way, I told him it was far too expensive. But being who he was, Dominic tracked down that jacket once we were back in the US and bought it. Made of wool, smooth and with a slight pile, soft to the touch, the jacket was a rich, saturated royal blue. He could certainly carry off a bold primary color. I eventually sent it to his nephew Christopher, who is tall and slender. I'm curious if it has ever been retailored for him or is in his closet as a keepsake. It was hard to let go of it.

His sister Donna asked if she could have his wedding ring back, as it had actually belonged to their father. She was very gracious in her request, realizing it might be difficult to let go, but I was happy to send it to her. He hadn't worn it in a while (his fingers gaining a little middle-aged weight?), and I had not invested much emotion in either of our rings. I wore mine for a while, but I never found rings very comfortable. His other jewelry I kept.

Then his shoes! Oh, Dominic! You loved shoes more than many women I know and the more expensive, the better. (There had definitely been some stealth shopping in our marriage.) I found one pair of ECCOs in the closet that he undoubtedly snuck by me and which had barely been worn. Again, who could I give a size 11 black leather loafer to who would appreciate the quality of the gift? His black terrycloth robe still hangs on the back of his closet door. In cooler weather, I occasionally wear it to the jacuzzi. It's long and thick and wraps me up completely. I haven't laundered it. I want to keep it feeling the way it does.

The contents of desks and drawers took more time. He had hundreds of 8 x 10 headshots for his work as an actor, taken at many different periods and sporting different looks. It was hard to see so many copies of his image in front of me, smiling up at me, looking directly at me, and then dump them in the garbage can.

And it didn't end there. His kitchen! After a few months, I realized I had way too many pots and pans, large pasta bowls, multiple gadgets and salad spinners. I mean, how many salad spinners do you really need? I was really grateful to have my friend Marta who liked organizing and took everything out of the drawers and cupboards and placed them on the kitchen island in categories. Then I came in and chose *one* of each category, or whatever I thought I might need for the can-opening and microwave-cooking I was most likely to execute.

Boxes and boxes of Christmas decorations were pulled from the garage closets and the contents reduced by at least a half. I couldn't face the idea of a Christmas without him. He had that playful spirit that I often lacked, that inner child that seemed to be missing in me. He loved putting up the tree every year (and yes, I did enjoy adding the pretty decorations, especially the ones that had memories from our overseas travels) and he made a whole little Christmas Village display in one of our alcoves. I wouldn't have had the patience. His favorite thing though was his train that went round the base of the Christmas tree. It whistled and puffed smoke. One time he went out and bought a newer and better Christmas Tree Train set, so I took the old one to the fire station for donation to a needy boy.

"Thank you," said the friendly fireman, "Has your little boy grown up?" I answered, "No, he just bought a bigger train."

One gift that was rewarding was the donation of his two guitars to a local high school in a not-too-affluent area. I was so glad that a music department would have two more instruments for students to use.

I still come across yellow sticky notes in his handwriting—odds and ends reminding him of phone calls he has to make or errands to be done. And the handwriting feels so intimate—it's like he just wrote the note. Those are the hardest to deal with as I come upon them unprepared, like rounding a corner and seeing someone you don't expect.

CHAPTER 15
APRIL: Showing Love with Food

April eventually rolled around, and I peeked more often out of my self-created cave. Outside, my paloverde tree was starting to bloom, and the jasmine was putting out its white flowers with their sweet fragrance.

Dominic's love of not only cooking for me but caring for me with food ended abruptly with his sudden death. Not only did I miss being spoiled with his amazing dishes, his slightly tipsy singing while cooking, and the smell of garlic being chopped, but I realized I would now have to feed myself, mainly food for sustenance. I could never replace the way he used food to care for me. He had filled my stomach and my heart at the same time, the two seeming intertwined.

One of the first things I needed to learn was how to go grocery shopping. This may seem like an obvious task that most adults know how to do, but I hadn't done grocery shopping in twenty years! (Some friends deemed me spoiled, but would you use the same epithet for a man whose wife did all the shopping?)

But my relationship with food had a strange background. Growing up in England, I never associated food with comfort. Food could be delicious, but its main function was the necessary one of fortifying the body so it could grow and be healthy. I never knew about cooking for fun. My paternal grandmother died many years before I was born so I had no warm memories of baking cookies with grandma. I have only the faintest images of the kitchen in my grandfather's old house, three hours north of us in the town of Worcester, England. I vaguely remember it had a real wood-burning fireplace, a couple of dogs, and Mary, a cheery British cook who had been with the family for years. Occasionally, I could visit there to taste from the latest collection of honeycombs brought in from my step-grandmother's bee hives. The sweetness of honey was a rare and precious memory from that kitchen. However, the family sat in the formal dining room for all meals. Houses at the time were not open concept, and kitchens, dining rooms, and living rooms were all entirely separate spaces intended for different activities.

Growing up as child, the kitchen in our own house in Tunbridge Wells was off-limits for kids, as, in the tradition at that time, we had a cook. So, hanging out in the kitchen was never an option. The kitchen was a place of work where the necessary job of meal preparation took place. Off the kitchen was a dark back stairway which twisted up to rooms I never saw, rooms I never visited. They were the private quarters of Mary, whom we addressed as "Cook", and her young son. Generally, my brother, sister, and I were fed early at 5 p.m., a meal called high tea. We couldn't join the evening meal until we were old enough to sit at the table, behave, and carry on an intelligent conversation. Perhaps I exaggerate with the intelligent conversation bit, but not by much.

Also, in England during the war, nearly all foods other than vegetables and bread were rationed. I don't ever remember going hungry, but we kept rabbits in the back garden, just in case we needed meat. My father, a doctor, whose creed was "Do No Harm," once was sent out to twist the neck of one of those cute white bunnies so we could have meat for dinner. He came back and told my mother, "I had a rough day at the hospital. I just can't do it today."

During the war, my other grandmother would send canned food supplies from Canada. "I feel guilty," said my mother "using them and having enough when our neighbors do not." Overindulgence or even the appearance of an excess of food was not considered a virtue. On the contrary, it was considered wasteful, and during the war years, waste was not tolerated. "If you're still hungry," my mother would say," have another piece of bread." In Canada (where we moved when I was 11), my grandparents were also quite formal and always had staff. No bonding over baking Christmas cookies occurred here, either. I don't even remember what their kitchen looked like. Christmas dinners were formal affairs where the service of dinner was so long and drawn out that we kids were given puzzles to keep us occupied between the passing around of the mashed potatoes and the Brussel sprouts by a staff member. Gravy came last.

My mother was not nearly so formal. However, she was not particularly fond of cooking and did it mainly to fulfill her role as a good 1950s "lady of the house." She never liked that role, she made that very clear. She sat at her little desk and wrote menus for the week but really wanted to be out painting a landscape. "Oh, I guess I have to go get something together for dinner tonight," she would say with absolutely no enthusiasm. She preferred her role as an artist. She hated making the Christmas fruitcake every year but plowed ahead with it, adding the bits of colored dried fruit and the dark brown raisins, all the while complaining about how much work it was. The concept of comfort food was foreign to me.

With two daughters, Mum tried to teach us the basics- -how to make a white sauce in the double boiler, for instance, and how to prepare vegetables in advance. At some point, my sister and I were assigned one dinner a week to prepare as part of our female education, though I was often dashing out to ballet class and throwing together my meal at the last moment. True to the gender roles of the time, I have no memory of my father *ever* preparing a meal or a dish for us to give Mum a break. As a doctor, he left early in the morning for the hospital, before we were even up. Once my mother died, he signed up for a cooking class as, he said "I haven't a clue."

I was thirty-five years old before I can remember the only time my father prepared and served food to me. I had returned home a few months after my mother's death and immediately came down with a terrible flu. In bed upstairs, I heard my father's footsteps coming up to the stairs. I was expecting Dad the Doctor to arrive to check in on me. Instead, he was bringing me a tray of breakfast. This was a first, and it made me uncomfortable. Ironically, later in life, it was always the men in my life who showed me love with food.

My first long-term (five-year) relationship was with a man called Bob, who soon learned that Hamburger Helper was at the high end of my repertoire and quickly took over all kitchen duties.

After marrying Dominic, I learned a whole new attitude towards food. Food was love, friends, comfort, conviviality, family, and fun. Everything revolved around the kitchen, where everyone inevitably gathered. The biggest fear in an Italian family is that there won't be enough, so more is bought and prepared. Excess is *encouraged.* I once was royally chewed out by Dominic for not providing food for a guest who had driven up from LA to visit us in Las Vegas. "Have you had lunch?" I had politely asked our guest when he arrived around 3 p.m. "Yes," he replied, so I thought nothing more about it since it was mid-afternoon. The next food offering would appear at dinner time. Was I wrong! Dominic was mortified when he arrived home a little later and heard I had fed poor Mickey nothing.

Cooking in Tuscany was even sweeter with fresh tomatoes from the garden

Dominic wears his apron from Spain

On another occasion, his first cousin John and his family were coming to spend a few days with us. This would be a chance for Dominic to show off not only our lovely house and his lovely wife but also his

93

most excellent Sauce, a sauce to rival all family sauces. The ingredients were assembled and sitting on the stove when he said, "Now it's time for me to shower, so keep an eye on the sauce for me, will you?" I took my responsibility seriously, and when I looked at the Sauce, it seemed like it was still cold and not bubbling, so I turned up the burner to full. When Dominic returned fresh and clean from his shower, the odor of burnt sauce filled the room. The sauce was burnt to a crisp, with a thick layer of brown across the bottom, and the disgusting flavor permeating the mixture, making it inedible. Not only didn't we have a pasta dinner to serve them, but I had totally disgraced him. As you can imagine, Dominic's horror and anger were of the highest order, and nothing I could do and no apologies made anything better. Not only had I ruined a brilliant sauce for Dominic's family members, but there was actually nothing to eat for dinner. At the time, I thought his rage was way out of proportion, but in retrospect, I realize I had not only damaged his pride but also ruined the centerpiece of a family occasion. I learned the hard way *never to turn up the heat again.*

I didn't even understand the concept of food for comfort in times of distress. On one occasion in LA, we got the news that the husband of a friend of ours had died, and that people were gathering at the widow's house.

"We must go right away," I said. Dominic had just made a big pot of sauce. "Shall we take the sauce?" he asked. I was horrified. "Dominic," I said with some indignation, "How can you think of food right now? C.J. needs comfort, not a plate of spaghetti."

I was so clueless.

Even before Dominic, I have always hated grocery shopping. One boyfriend I had in my single days in the 1970s used to bring a sandwich when he would drop over, as he said all he could find in my fridge was a bottle of vodka and a steak.

If I had to restock, I usually chose a small independent grocery shop, as I liked to get in and out quickly. If I could resupply my kitchen within ten minutes, I would be a happy camper.

On the other hand, Dominic loved grocery shopping. He went up and down every single aisle. He knew all the grocery clerks in every store, especially Trader Joe's, and they all knew him. Eventually, because I was working full- time with very long hours, he completely took over the task. He made it a full-time, joy-filled activity on his chosen day. He started at the other end of Las Vegas at the International Food Market, getting specialty items, then went to the Italian store to get his Italian products (only a certain kind of canned tomato was deemed worthy), then traveled on to a big box store to get paper products, and journeyed lastly to Trader Joes to get produce and his wine, at an excellent price.

Now he was gone, I had to face the grocery store again. It seemed even more daunting than ever, with aisles twice as long, the choices overwhelming, and I seemed to have shrunk to a tiny, bewildered little girl. I can find the eggs and the milk, but why is there an entire mile of cereals, and how do I choose? Where on earth are the capers? Are they vegetables, tiny fruit, or condiments? I dash in and out, purchase the bare essentials, and if I forget something, I won't go back to find it, at least until the next time I brave a grocery store.

The year of COVID-19 saved me from total embarrassment. I could now order my groceries online and have them delivered, guilt-free. I would be helping the locals who had lost their jobs in the Las Vegas casinos and hotels and were desperate for tips of any kind. I could tell my friends this guaranteed less exposure to unknown germs, and less risk of infecting others. The safest grocery shopping was not *in* the store among other germy people, but having groceries delivered by a single brave soul wearing a mask.

"Don't you want to pick out your own avocados?" my friends asked incredulously. "How do you know they won't bring you wilted lettuce or sour grapes?"

I felt incredibly guilty. Many of my friends go to Costco to save fifty cents on a box of oranges. How wasteful am I? But here's the thing, if you get past the idea that you are going to be judged by others or your critical self, it can be a joy. Go online, where all the goods are listed with cost, calorie information, and cute little pictures. Add it to your cart. Select a time for delivery or pick up, and voila, you're all done. I pay an annual fee for the service, which, when divided up into weekly deliveries, is very modest indeed.

In my community of seniors, we often go out to eat. It's one of the rewards of a life well lived… to be able to go to different restaurants, be ushered to a table, served water, then wine, and asked what we would like to eat. "My name is Tony, and I will be taking care of you today." How nice is that! Happy Hour was originally invented to lure white-collar office workers in for a quick martini or two after work and before they head to the commuter train to get home, but it is now the senior set's purview. We love to get to a bar early (between 4 and 5 p.m., though I prefer 5 p.m.), where we benefit from quick seating, half-price drinks, and "small plates," which serve as dinner if you eat enough of them. Yes, we are home by 7 p.m. and in bed with TV or a book by 9:30 p.m. Yes, this is the life of the Retirement Set.

I probably will never associate food with comfort the way Dominic or my Italian in-laws did, but now I at least can associate it with fun with friends, and the freedom from having to make a meal. So perhaps food is still love, or at least friendship. Mangia!

Dominic, in his happy place, our kitchen

CHAPTER 16
FROM SHIT BROWN TO BABY BLUE:
Time to redecorate

One of the first steps in my recovery was to reinvent my physical space.

When faced by any loss, there's no point in trying to hold on to what was. It's best to welcome the space that opens up and fill it with something new. A few years before his death, Dominic decided the abundance of Las Vegas Beige on every wall was too much for him. "We need an accent wall," he said, and I agreed. Off to work I went and returned to one large wall painted rust with a slight sheen to it. I liked it. Our living room sofa set was dark brown leather and worked well with the new color. My taste was very different from his—much lighter and brighter. However, I always felt that part of being married was to try to compromise on things, and some battles were not worth fighting. Besides, I got to go and do the work that I loved and come back to a home-cooked meal, so it seemed like an okay arrangement.

This was one of the few big compromises I made in our marriage. I often wished he could be one of those husbands who said, "Darling, just do whatever you want. I have no understanding of interior design." I thought since I was a costume designer and understood color and textiles and shape, my opinion would count for a lot. But he also had strong opinions. I considered myself lucky that I got my way in most other areas -- where we went on vacation and when, what movie we would see on Sunday, even what I wanted for dinner. So, I let him win when it came to the look of our home's interior.

A few months later, he said, "The rust wall is too dominating, I think we need another wall painted." I agreed. He was really good at prepping for a job, doing it, and bless him, clearing up after himself, a series of talents I had not achieved, at least in household chores. Again, I went to work and returned to the opposite wall painted a luminous gold color. It looked pretty good. He was right! But the large living room needed something to tie it all together, so I made some curtains in the same rust color.

Next, he painted our bedroom and bathroom blue. I like blue, but they turned out to be so bright, we could hardly sleep. It felt like a school room that should have cutout giraffes of orange and yellow poster paper and other brightly colored playful animals on the walls. He realized it, too. Back to the paint chips. The only color left in this limited set of luminous paints was brown. Brown!!! "Like a copper penny," he said. Brown, indeed. I hate brown, but brown it was, so I swear I am the only person on earth (other than natives in mud huts) to sleep in a shit-brown bedroom.

On my own, I can finally repaint. I chose a cornflower blue that feels like spring. It's glorious. On the walls, I hung a collection of small watercolors I collected on my travels, all, not surprisingly, from warm climates. I have the Pont D'Avignon from sunny southern France, a whitewashed street in Mykonos, and a stiltwalker from St Croix. I also hung a lovely print by the artist Shari Erickson called "Secret Sisters," of four lovely women and a child on the beach in Antigua, wearing bright dresses and holding colorful umbrellas. I adore this picture.

My friend Ilene, a brilliant interior decorator, took me shopping to find new bedside tables and a chest of drawers. We found the chest and a bedside table. But I need two, I thought. No, she said, there is no real reason you have to have a bedside table on each side of the bed. That's when it hit me - there would be no one in the opposite side of the bed with me. Even though the thought hurt, it did save me several hundred dollars on a second table and lamp.

I decided next that the rust wall and the gold wall in the living room had to go. Instead, I had a lovely pale shade of grey painted all through the living room and into the kitchen. An off-white sofa replaced the brown leather one. My Tamara de Lempicka canvas was hung on a wall in the kitchen and looked so different on the light-colored background that reflected the grey in the painting. The woman's red lipstick in the painting adds a touch of accent color, which I never noticed before in its old location.

I added some Moroccan touches in the sunroom to go with the antique Moroccan octagonal table my grandparents bought in the 1920's, which I treasure, even though it is sadly in need of restoration. And so, bit by bit, I recreated my space, more open, more light, more feminine. The house became more mine and less ours. It was a bittersweet feeling.

CHAPTER 17
TRAVEL: Without Dominic

I have never been afraid of traveling alone. At age ten, I traveled across the Atlantic Ocean with only my twelve-year-old brother as an escort, to be met by our grandparents on the other side. As an eighteen-year-old college student, I took the two-day train across Canada by myself to my summer job in Banff Springs. The trip was a grand adventure.

But these trips were to go from point A to point B. They were not intrinsically trips for pleasure or vacation. The summer after Dominic died, I felt the need to travel to fill my time and, perhaps, my emptiness. I had mourned all winter and spring, and now, I was at the stage where I wanted to get away from the house we had shared and the memories it held. In June, after he died, I visited friends for a week in Depoe Bay on the northwest Pacific Coast and spent a week in August with other friends in downtown Honolulu. I visited my in-laws in Buffalo and my siblings in Toronto. Now I just wanted to get away. For *me*.

I didn't want to worry about what kind of a brave front I was putting on, or field questions about "how are you *really* doing?" I wanted a few days to only please myself and be myself with no one watching me.

I wanted to wake up in the morning somewhere warm, the sky blue and sunny, and where I could jump into the most turquoise water I could find. I chose Great Exuma , one of more than 365 islands east of Florida in the outer Bahamas, before the shallow water falls off into the vast Atlantic Ocean. I rented a small one-bedroom cabin right on the beach. It was part of a modest resort, mainly catering to families. It sat on the one narrow road that ran the length of the island. There were no shops or cafes close enough to walk to, but on-site, there was a bar and restaurant where the food was simple but adequate. At first, the location met all my requirements. The beaches were indeed deserted, the breezes gentle, and swimming in the crystal clear, warm, and pale aqua water did my soul good. I knew no one and saw no one, but I still felt relatively safe. The locals all knew each other and seemed way too laid back to bother about attacking or robbing me. One local told me that if one of them saw me on the beach, they'd move to another beach, considering mine was too crowded!

Alone on the beach in Exuma

But there was no sugarcoating it, I was sometimes very lonely. The restaurant was full of families, who, while friendly when I smiled and said good morning, were not inclined to speak to me further. I had what I thought I wanted. Freedom, anonymity. But on the second morning, I cried for an hour. I missed Dominic, my sister, my cat, and my friends back home and wondered why I had put myself on a small strip of sand in the middle of nowhere. Worst of all, that morning, the Wi-Fi, only available in a certain corner of the lobby, was down, so I couldn't even call my friend Roula. But the feeling passed.

Things are very mellow in the Exumas, and nothing works quite right, but it doesn't seem to matter. The only clock in the resort was thirty minutes slow, and pretty soon, I slowed too. I swam a fair amount and took a lot of naps. I didn't exclude tourism altogether. I booked a half-day boat tour to see the now-famous swimming pigs. Another day, I rode into the small town of George Town to catch Elvis's Water Taxi to Stocking Island. Elvis's small boat looked like it had been dredged up from a shipwreck and never renovated, but it went back and forth all day every hour with no problem. It cost $5, and he said he would make sure someone picked me up and brought me back before the day's end.

I visited the famous Chat' n Chill beach bar on Stocking Island. Ordering my usual vodka and lime, I sat at the bar alone. No one else was around until a gorgeous blond woman arrived, tall, shapely, and in a very skimpy bikini! She soon attracted three or four men, in their early 40's, who hung all over her and lapped up her stories of dumping her no-good boyfriend. One of the men was on the stool next to me, and as he gradually spun around to focus on this lovely trollop, he created a large wall with his back and shoulders, squeezing me into a relatively tight space. Soon, the mens' wives showed up and stood behind or near their men, observing the boys making fools of themselves. Then our blond bombshell said, "I don't mind traveling alone. I always make friends wherever I go." With perhaps a note of resentment in my voice, I piped up, "Easy for you to say when you are thirty years old and slim, not so easy when you are my age."

One of the wives immediately saw my plight and came up to talk to me and make me part of the group. Bless her, she was my beach rescue angel, and I will never forget her.

My travel to the Exumas didn't provide any major epiphany about facing aloneness, other than that I can do it if I have to. Sometimes, you need the quiet, the lack of structure, the beauty, and mostly the time to breathe, cry, sleep, and swim to get to the next level of healing. And Exuma gave me just that.

Once back home and gradually settling into my new life as a single person, I confronted that thought that so many widows have, who will I travel with now? Dominic and I started traveling within six months of our meeting and did well together. We both had a rather hedonistic attitude toward travel. Don't show me all the things I need to see and learn, just give me a good table at a sidewalk café, and let me eat and drink well, and people watch!

Perhaps I could travel with girlfriends, but I didn't have any then. I had my one remaining high school and university friend, but she was married with kids and grandkids, and lived in Toronto. My dear friend and fellow dancer Elinor, who I had toured with in *My Fair Lady* and shared an apartment with in New York City, died young from a brain disease. A few others here and there were married or lived miles away (even one in Australia). I could think of no travel candidates. None.

But I loved to hang out on my computer on VRBO and similar sites and daydream about the villas on hilltops in Tuscany, or on the shores of the Amalfi Coast, or among the blue waters of the Caribbean. One day, I discovered a house on the Caribbean island of Antigua. Sitting on a hilltop, it had a magnificent view over Jolly Harbor and its collection of sailboats and catamarans. Across the front of the house was a long verandah with comfy furniture where I envisioned sitting and gazing out at the sunset while sipping my favorite vodka drink. Down some steps was a pool with an infinity edge, and I could see how, once in it, the water of the pool would merge splendidly with the color of the ocean water. Bougainvillea were everywhere, one of my favorite flowers, reminding me of when I first saw them at age eighteen in southern France. Each of the four bedrooms had lovely cool decor with blues and greens, and light coming through shutters or sheer curtains. It looked like heaven on earth. But it was $486 a day. There was no way I could ever afford to go there. Or was there? Maybe, just maybe, I could find some people to go with me and share the cost. I went on the old baseball movie adage, "If you build it, they will come." I took a leap of faith and put a deposit on it, knowing I would have seven months to find people to share it or cancel for a refund.

Without a moment's hesitation, the first person to sign on was one of my neighbors, who I knew was single and with whom I had gone to various events within my community. I was astounded when she said yes.

The next thing I knew, she had asked a friend of hers if she was interested and wanted to see if I was okay with extending an invitation to her. The word was out! Two more signed on, and just when we were a full house of five, one more person came over and begged me to let her come too, even though it meant a second car and more shared bedrooms. I was ecstatic. Now I had a way to afford this divine house on the hill, and I also had girlfriends to go with me. I was, of course, nervous about how this would turn out. I was not especially close with any of the women, and yet I felt that as single women, all widows, they would relish the opportunity to go somewhere exotic and share the experience. And it turned out pretty well! Other than one friend getting bitten all over by mosquitoes that entered the house due to the negligence of another woman leaving a door open, or the slight kerfuffle when the TV in the main living area was tuned to a right-wing channel without checking the political leanings of the group as a whole first, we had a great time. We swam in our pool, visited the local restaurants, and went to St. John for shopping. Since then, I have done a lot of traveling in this style, and I like it.

I have only experienced one giant cruise ship, an experience that was not for me. I found myself bored—yes, bored—as the weather was lousy, and we couldn't go in the pool, and the ports of call all seemed to offer the same limited, tourist-oriented shops, eateries, and excursions. Plus, I didn't enjoy lining up for the buffet or taking a number to get a tender into port. At one island, six other giant cruise ships were visiting at the same time, too many to come into port, so we were anchored a few miles down the coast and were ferried into shore, whereupon we had to wait for vans to come and pick us up and take us to town. In town, we fought our way through the crowds that had descended upon the island at the same time, all vying for seats at the same port-side restaurants and clogging up the narrow walkways. Before long, it was time to reverse the process and catch the van back, the tender out, to be back on board by departure time. Not my style of travel.

But the small group experience, staying locally, yes. I learned that it is important to gauge each person's rhythms when planning this kind of group travel. Some are early risers, some late. Some like to hang out and go slow, others can't wait to get going and see things. There are many ways to ensure everyone gets to do what they like and at the pace they enjoy. With each trip, I learn more about how to have a successful vacation, merging five (occasionally six) personalities and needs. And being a people pleaser, there is always that element of anxiety, "I hope they have a good time."

I am not a big fan of hotels for vacations, especially with a group of people. I want to avoid finding myself in my bedroom wondering what everyone else is up to and if they have all gone down for dinner and forgotten to tell me. With a combined house, condo, or villa, you can all gather in the common space to enjoy company before the day's activities and at the end of the day. And I can go to bed early if I so desire and know I won't be alone in the morning.

The other issue that my age has forced me to confront is that I can no longer lift heavy weights, meaning my luggage has to be no more than thirty lbs. I have trained myself to pack no more than that in either a carry-on or a duffle bag, along with a backpack of no more than ten pounds. This is a fact of life. I am not strong anymore, though I try to maintain my upper body strength. Packing large suitcases with umpteen choices of clothes and shoes just doesn't make sense for me. It hurts to lift them up onto the scales at check in, it's a pain to drag them a mile and a half down the concourse, and it's a struggle to lift them up into the overhead bin. In my opinion, getting old does not have to be the end of travel. If travel is important to you, it just needs managing. I know that as I age, and mobility and stamina become more of an issue, I will need to plan even more carefully. But I will not stop traveling.

CHAPTER 18
Who Is Left To Touch Me?

These days I am seldom embraced or held or touched by another human being. Being widowed and childless leads me to this awful consideration, I wonder if I will ever again be fully embraced. Will I feel that hug, cheek to cheek, chest to chest, hips to hips, all the way down? What I call a full-body hug. None of that polite triangular avoiding-hip-touching thing.

Dominic and I used to spoon before we went to sleep. I felt the weight of his body in the bed next to me and then felt him roll over until his chest was next to my back, and he put his arm across my body. His skin was soft against mine. I could feel the faint warmth of his breath, and his heart beating. His bent knees fit nicely into the crook of my knees. In this blissful state of being cradled, I fell asleep instantly. During the day, there was always a kiss goodbye when one of us was about to leave the house to go on our day's activities. "When will you be home?" was always the question, and we would always have an answer, so the other person knew what to expect. I cherish that kiss I gave him the morning I left for work, never to see him alive again. "See you tonight, honey."

When one of us went away on business or to see family, the other was always at the airport to provide the welcome back. Riding down the escalator toward baggage claim, my heart quickened as I saw him there waiting, a big grin on his face, waiting to give me a heartfelt kiss. Only then to the business of hauling luggage off the carousel or discussing that the washing machine had broken down while I was away.

Until you lose your husband, your lover, you never think about these embraces. Or your lips. It never occurred to me that my lips touching a man's lips would be an experience that ended with him. All my five senses long for him. As a single woman, and not anticipating another lover or husband, I wonder, will I ever feel the touch of a man again? Has anyone talked about the loss of tactile experience as we age? I know people talk about the need for babies to be held. Volunteers go into neo-natal units and hold and rock the babies. But what about the senior population? Do the experts in aging realize that we are touched less and less as we age? Perhaps we have the occasional hugs of siblings when we see them (and how often is that?), and many, of course, have the touch of children and grandchildren. I don't have that.

As babies, we are touched all the time. We are laid on our mother's chest the moment we are out of the womb. Held, cuddled, fed, changed, snuggled, looked at eye to eye. In Bali, I am told babies are held for the first six months of their life and never touch the ground. As toddlers, we are also touched a great deal, sometimes to hold us back from getting ourselves into trouble, sometimes to comfort us when we fall or bump our heads.

For older kids, touching continues with rough house, playtime, and rolling around laughing. As teens, we become a bit more shy about being touched. " Mo…om!" As young adults, we explore being touched by others, especially those we are attracted to. The first kiss. And so on— until middle to old age, when the touching becomes less frequent. And when one's partner goes, who is left to touch us?

I think we are beings created with the sense of touch for a reason. How can we fulfill that need as we age? I don't know, to be honest. Perhaps we too need volunteers, men or women to come in and just hug us, long and hard, no questions asked.

During the two years of COVID-19, touching became forbidden and dangerous. Hugging was verboten. Fist bumps replaced handshakes. Since the Me-Too movement, touching can also be risky. You might have to ask permission to touch another human. As a costume designer, I now ask permission to touch before throwing a measuring tape around an actor's chest. Nobody ever thought twice about that before.

So how to be touched? It's no wonder I like massages so much. Not that a massage is touching that is in any way sexual, romantic, or even mildly affectionate. It is a clinical and therapeutic touch. But I still enjoy it immensely. I love the feel of my cat, whom I love to touch way more than she loves to be touched. Her fur is soft, and her white belly is warm when she offers it to me. I would bury my face in her fur if she'd let me, but the exchange of affection pretty much has to be on her terms.

But the feel of a man? I may have to face the fact that I may never experience that feeling again in the years to come.

A few years after Dominic's death, I began to think I needed to be in the company of a male from time to time, so I joined Match.com. Maybe I could be touched gently, carefully, a little at a time. Was it possible?

At first, it was an adventure, as it gave me a sense of power to be the chooser, but I found that the selection of men in their 70s and 80s was not that great. Perhaps they were looking for younger women. Let's look first at the photos the men posted. Now, none of us are young and hot anymore, so who is kidding who? But there were photos of men with baseball caps, cowboy hats, fishermen's bucket hats. Men standing in front of the sink in the bathroom in their tank tops. Beards and bellies. Nose hair. No hair. Unkempt hair.

My first date was with a reasonably nice-looking man, but I was highly suspicious that he was using a photo from his younger days. When I met him, he walked slowly with a cane (which could have been Okay), but I realized that sooner rather than later, he might need a nurse with a purse—not me.

Another man took me for iced tea and proceeded to tell me about his life, his kids, his illnesses, his aches and pains, his loneliness, and after a while, I wondered when he was going to say, "And how about you, Diana, tell me about yourself." When I realized that wasn't going to happen, I made a little game of it and thought I would time how long it took before he turned his attention to me. It was forty-five minutes. Then it was back to him and how difficult it was to find a companion and how much he wanted to go on a cruise with someone. I thought to myself, "Dear God, I'd rather stick pins in my eyes than go on a cruise with you."

Another man agreed to take me to the movies, and asked me to choose the movie. So far, so good. But he fell asleep within the first five minutes of the movie, never to revive until the lights came back on. (Yes, the movie did suck, but I managed to stay awake.)

Another man met me for a cocktail at Bob Taylor's Ranch House, which I thought was a fun and unique place to meet. As we walked out to the parking lot afterward, he said, "Well, I hope you find what you are looking for." Oh, my, in other words," Have a nice life, and I'm not interested. " Hmmm, I hadn't thought that he might be the chooser, too. I thought I was the chooser.

I canceled my subscription to Match.com, only to re-subscribe about two years later. I decided to try again. Was there someone out there for me? Though my girlfriends all offered to make the escape phone call, I didn't have any trouble in Round One of the dates. However, for Round Two, I thought it advisable to sign up with a background check website and check out possible suitors for anything fishy—prison stays, DUIs, double lives, and Ponzi schemes. I tried it out on my next date and quickly searched his name. Very strange. Nothing on his record made any sense. There were multiple aliases, and there were possible links to a criminal background. This man seemed the nicest, quietest, and least harmful man I could possibly imagine, but then looks can deceive, can't they? He could be the quiet axe murderer we have all been worried about. Eventually, I wrote a text to him explaining that I was having trouble verifying him. I hoped that he understood that as a single woman I was being careful. He couldn't have been more gracious about it, saying that he understood and would advise his three daughters to do the same thing if they were dating.

However, I had his name wrong. It wasn't Ben. It was Bill. Oops! He teased me about it a couple of times when we went on dates, saying he was sorry Ben couldn't show up, but Bill was here in his absence. Bill was a lovely man and a gentleman, too, but there was just no spark. I didn't see any value in prolonging things.

At some point, I realized I might be opening myself to actually *liking* someone or even being *attracted* to them. Could I really go back to that? The "I hope he calls, why hasn't he called?" jitters. "He said he would call, it's been three days already. It's been a week already, I guess he's not going to call." The drama, and then feeling like shit. I remember those days all too well.

With each contact I made, I thought "This one may spark an interest." I always had high hopes for some reason. And the last one on my Match period was the doozy. He seemed ideal for me. Formerly married to an English dancer, then widowed, loved going to the ballet, etc. A match made in heaven, right? What could possibly go wrong? My friend and dating coach told me to "stay light, smile, and don't get too much into your head." When I sat down at the booth in the restaurant we had chosen, and he said "Oh, you look just like your photo," I smiled and said, "I hope that's a good thing," silently congratulating myself that I had made a little self-deprecating joke.

All went well at first, though he mentioned how often he dated and more stories of other relationships, more than I thought appropriate on a first date. Then he told me that after two dinners out with a new woman, he liked to cook for her at his house. He described in some lavish detail the menu, including the courses and choices of wine, and I began to realize that, should I get to date number three with him, I too might be on the menu as an after-dinner treat of some kind. I was getting the signal that sex was expected. Then, as I sat there listening to all this, he told me he had just met a woman and had accepted her invitation to go on a cruise with her, but he was only meeting with me in case that didn't work out. I'm in the lineup, on stand-by, and next in line?

I was a bit dumbfounded. I looked for a way out. One option was to pick up my purse and say I was heading for the lady's room and then head out to my car and home. But that seemed a bit passive-aggressive. The other choice was to blithely munch away on my tilapia and spinach entree and know that eventually the date would end and I could go home to my cat, who loved me and totally accepted me for me. Oh wait, she expects dinner and a rub, too.

When I recounted this to my Match coach, Roula, she said there was a third choice. Why didn't I just say, as soon as I knew, "Excuse me, I don't think this is going to work out, so I'll leave now." and then exit with a bit of dignity? As she said this, I burst into tears as I suddenly realized I had been disrespected by this man in a very oblique way, and I had reverted to my insecure, thirteen-year-old self, knowing something was wrong and not knowing how to handle it. He wasn't really doing anything terrible except being a jerk, but it brought back every occasion, minor or major where I sat dumbfounded in the past, not being able to put thoughts into words. It even reminded me of situations where I had been inappropriately touched by people in power during my days as a young dancer and remained polite and long-suffering instead of giving the guy a slap across the face. I was angry at myself. I wondered why I was not more mature and in tune with my feelings. Good god, Diana, you are supposed to be a mature adult! I felt humiliated, as much by my inability to articulate my feelings and choose an appropriate way out, as by my inability to articulate them.

Then there was Robert. In our first phone call, I asked him if he preferred Robert, Rob, or Bob. "Wobert, "he answered. It was all I could do not to snort with laughter! Now, I am a well-brought-up woman and know it is not nice to mock people's limitations, but given the choices and the problem with pronunciation, don't you think he'd opt for Bob? So that ended my go-around with Match.

Dating as an oldster is bloody difficult. When you are young, you are at your best looking, pheromones buzzing, and you catch a look with a man across the room. Physical attraction definitely comes first. You hope his brain will be okay, but really, at this point, who cares? Eventually, you find yourself in the same corner talking, and before long, you establish that you want to see each other. With Dominic, I looked into his dark eyes and admired his long black eyelashes as we barely spoke while conducting business. He was at my workplace (Bob Mackie's atelier) to pick up a load of boxes of costumes to transport to Las Vegas for the show "Jubilee", and I was directing which costumes were ready for transport.

When Dominic came to my house for our first date, it was lust at first sight. Once he crossed my threshold, he never left for the next 35 years. Physical attraction came first, and personality attraction came later. And then love. Much love (sigh).

But how will this happen when one 79-year-old is looking at photos of other 79-year-olds, many of whom don't know how to take a good selfie? And maybe they haven't exercised since the Bush presidency, and don't even get me started about men who take their picture in a tank top in their bathroom! It's not quite a dick pic, but perhaps the oldster version? Would I send a photo of me in my bra?

What do I want? Do I want a relationship or not? That, as Hamlet said, is the question. The difficult thing is to first *decide* what you are really looking for and then project that on your profile (one man called it my "ad"). The profile is an outline at best. Are you divorced or widowed? Have children or not? Are you religious or not? Do you have political leanings?

I think now that I don't want to re-marry, but who knows?

I think now that I want to stay in my own house, not move in with anyone else, but who knows?

I think now that sex is definitely out of the question, but who really knows? I hate to admit that I have completely lost interest in sex. I hate saying it as it lowers me on my own "cool" scale. I'd love to say, "I am a feisty old broad who loves a romp in the hay as well as anyone," but shoot, it's just not true.

When I date men from Match of whom I've only seen some poorly taken selfies, and had an initial phone call, do I even bring this up? Do I try and find out if the old duffer I'm about to have dinner with is also over sex and doesn't want it either? Do I alert him that bedding me is a very distant thing and he shouldn't waste his time?

When I picture myself going to bed with a new man, it is not the nudity part that worries me. I have never been shy about my body, probably from all those years as a dancer where leotards and tights showed it all and costumes for performance could be skimpy. No, it is the thought of those elements of intimacy that I simply cannot imagine with another person. The heavy breathing sounds of the body next to you, the flushing of the toilet during the night, the apologies for the snoring, the embarrassment of waking up to an unfamiliar face. It's just all too ghastly to imagine, and it in no way sounds appealing.

What about a new app, a dating site similar to The Voice, where there is a blind audition? On this app, you can chat back and forth via text and get to know each other's tastes and sense of humor before being put off or loving the potential candidate's appearance?

Or here's another idea for a new dating app--in the column where you enter your choice of Woman Seeking Man, or Woman Seeking Woman, etc., I wish there was a choice of Woman Seeking Gay Man! Wouldn't that be great! A companion who would know who Stephen Sondheim was, who would like to go to the ballet, who notices when you are wearing a designer dress and would make you feel like the most *amazing* woman in the world! And all this without wanting sex!! My gay friends have always been funny, full of life, and made me feel adored.

His ad would read: Gay man seeks straight woman. Must be attractive, but not more so than I. Must love Diana Ross. No sex required. I can be extremely loyal, even as our looks fade, and will make you laugh until your last day.

CHAPTER 19
MONEY MATTERS: The Feeling of Being Poor

The moment a spouse dies, I discovered, all sorts of money matters change. I was immediately down $2000 a month in income. I would not have Dominic's income from *Tony n'Tina's Wedding* or his Social Security check—his first one was due to arrive the month that he died. On the other side of the coin, I had a small life insurance policy on him, which dropped into my bank account with surprising ease after some papers were signed, unlike the complicated procedure of getting the utility bills changed over to my name and out of his. Dominic and I had decided to take out life insurance on each other some years back. Of course, it was assumed that I would die first, and so a larger amount was placed on me, knowing that he would need money to survive for many more years once I died.

How much money you *have* and how you *feel* about it has much to do with how you grew up around money. I have always felt poor. Now, get up off the floor and stop laughing. I know, I know. How can I possibly say I feel poor when I grew up in a privileged household, went to private schools, and had every advantage a young person could want to start their life? Though it is easy to blame everything on one's mother or father, in this case, I think my fear of being deathly poor did, in fact, come from my parents. I am not angry about it. I don't think they meant to convey this. But they instilled a deep fear in me that I would never have enough, let alone experience abundance. This left me always feeling unsafe at a gut level.

My father came from a well-established, old-money family in England as did my mother in Canada. But old money is often different from what you might expect. In my experience, it comes with a very strict Protestant conservatism and all sorts of rules about appreciating the value of money, earning your way, not having expectations, and so forth. Add to this the fact that my parents endured hard times in England during the war (yes, that one, WW2) and then, in 1951, emigrated to my mother's birthplace, Toronto, Canada, to start a new life with all its economic risks. My father had to study and take his medical exams all over again to get his licenses, as his British ones were no good in Canada for some reason. That meant that for a long time there was no income, nor could they bring cash with them from England.

For my mother especially, this was very hard, as she returned to Toronto no longer the debutante and socially prominent young woman she had left as. She returned with three children and a man with no income, to a city where the social strata were clearly established. Her old friends were all happily ensconced in large homes in the best areas of town, with summer homes and memberships in the right clubs. As teenagers, when one is totally selfish and sees only one's needs, my siblings and I were being told, "No, you can't have this," and "No, you can't have that; we can't afford it." Money spent on us, on my dancing lessons, for instance, always felt like it was costing my parents in a painful way. There was an expression my dad used, along with a forlorn face, "We must tighten our belts," which, when you think about it, means that you don't have enough to eat and your trousers fall down from loss of weight.

In twelfth grade, all but three of my class went to Bermuda for Spring Break. Mum and Dad said I could have ballet classes *or* a trip to Bermuda, but not both. So, I didn't go. One of the three "poor kids" who didn't go. Of course, in retrospect, as an adult, I totally get it. With limited resources, the portion allotted to me was all used up with my dance classes. There also had to be money for my brother and sister's extra-curricular needs.

I had my first summer job at fifteen, and every summer after that, as did my brother and sister. After an excellent university education, I chose a career in the arts, which are rarely known for being lucrative except for a rare few. In my twenties, in New York City, I had a stellar career as a dancer in Broadway shows, and concede that I was successful in how many shows I was cast in at the highest level. But the chorus pay was low, just enough to pay for my fourth-floor walk-up apartment and basic living expenses. During those weeks and months in between shows, I relied on unemployment insurance (my father called it "the dole") and some odd jobs to get me through. There was no way to save for the future. Once in Los Angeles, I also lived in a gig economy. For four years, during the fading years of my acting career, I worked as a cocktail waitress and supplemented that meager income by sewing patchwork pillows and quilts. As I got going and became a successful, working costume designer in TV shows and films, I would just get ahead when my series would get canceled, and I would be back where I started, careful with every dollar. It was a very insecure profession financially, even though I earned well during the months I was employed.

This lifestyle did nothing to help me overcome the feeling of potential financial disaster. This worry of always being poor continues to exist somewhere in the deep recesses of my brain. I still have nightmares from time to time about having $20 left to my name and not knowing how I am going to make it. I have always bought with a poor mindset. If I buy a new Apple iPhone I always buy two models down from the latest release. I buy things on sale. I never buy anything of top quality. Dominic had to sneak new shoes into his closet and hope that I didn't notice and give my standard, "How can you be buying new shoes when you already have twelve pairs?" In fact, Dominic and I were so different on this. He had this blissful belief that everything would somehow take care of itself and there would always be enough. Enough? What a concept.

If only we knew how long we would live—then I would divide what I have by the number of years left and spend it all. My insurance agent once estimated that my expected departure date would be at 89-years-old, and I am only four years away from that. Now, I think I am going to live well into my nineties and possibly, God forbid, into my hundreds. I worry I could never have enough for retirement, and for all the possible health care issues, nursing care homes, or unexpected emergencies that might arise. What if I outlive my savings? The idea of having to make less-than-ideal choices because of lack of funds, or to not have a choice at all, often terrifies me.

A few years after Dom's death, my financial advisor Christopher, called and said, "You know Diana, you can start spending down your account." I didn't even know what this meant and asked him to explain. "If you don't spend it, your nieces and nephews named in your will get it, so why not you?"

He assured me that as long as I didn't go crazy with new spending, I could spend more out of my account. I hung up the phone and sat for a minute to digest this. A huge weight had been lifted off my shoulders and created a new sense of ease I had not experienced before. Gingerly, like a lion finally released from a lifelong cage, I tip-toed out of that cage and tested his theory that I could spend a little more and not throw my future into danger.

This has really impacted my old age and my enjoyment of it. The frequency of my travels these last few years has been a direct result of being freer with my money. Now in my eighties I am taking three to four trips a year, knowing that my time is limited and my stamina for long plane rides diminishing yearly. "Where are you off to next?" my young friends ask me and I am happy to inform them of my next exotic destination. "I want to be you when I grow up," these young adults say playfully. We spend so much saving for that fearful future, that future where we imagine all sorts of terrible things happening, that we don't enjoy our third and final stage of life. As long as I don't have some terrible disease not covered by insurance or some unforeseen natural disaster that demolishes my house, I think I'll be okay.

In trying to accept this new attitude towards spending on myself (and others, but mostly, I confess, myself!) I read the book *Die With Zero: Getting All You Can from Your Money and Your Life* by Bill Perkins. It presents a provocative philosophy that went against everything I had been taught, *Plan, save, plan, save. The future is unknown and scary.* The author presents the idea that the money saved that will follow you to your grave is wasted money, money that could have brought you memorable experiences while you were alive. The author suggests that you have wasted far too many hours of your life acquiring money if you don't enjoy it and spend it before you die. In other words, you should aim to "Die With Zero."

So I am trying to find a happy medium. I think back to my mother's semi-annual shopping list columns, "Have", "Need", and "Want". Right now, I want fun, friends, good food, travel, and the ability to buy things on those travels that are totally and ridiculously unnecessary if I desire them. I'm about to turn eighty-years-old, and Godammit, there is plenty on my "Want" list.

It's now or never!

PART TWO

CHAPTER 20
TURNING EIGHTY: A Spectacular Celebration

When I turned eighty, I thought it was a huge deal. I wanted to plan a spectacular celebration with friends and family. I wanted money to be spent with wild abandon. I treated it as if no one had *ever* turned eighty before.

I guess I was shocked that it was happening. I mean, I didn't have an image of myself as an eighty-year-old. I'd managed to accept seventy years and then, reluctantly, seventy-five.

But eighty? That was old.

What was eighty really going to be like? How would I be? Was this the beginning of the end, the last vestiges of usefulness, of energy, of any kind of good looks? Was it just a waiting game until I went into the next world? Would I just be marking time until I fell off the perch? Until I just disappeared altogether?

I have few examples in my immediate family of what it's like to be eighty or older. Both my parents died before age seventy-five, my paternal grandmother died before I was born, and my maternal grandmother died in her mid-seventies.

I wanted to plan and produce this milestone birthday celebration, even if I had to do it all myself. Some of my traveling girlfriends from the neighborhood had been talking about a week's sightseeing trip to Washington, DC. "Why not combine it with a birthday celebration for me?" I queried. With their agreement, I went to my favorite site, VRBO (or was it Airbnb?), and found us a lovely old house that could sleep six, located on Capitol Hill near Eastern Market. We would be sightseers during the week, visiting several of the museums, and then on the final Saturday, I arranged for a private room in the famous Hay-Adams Hotel for my dinner party.

Then my siblings wanted to come too. My sister and husband (and two dogs) would drive up from Florida and stop over only if I could find suitable pet-friendly accommodations for them. My brother and wife were going to drive down from Toronto. Then, my two favorite nieces agreed to shirk their jobs and motherly duties (leaving husbands and kids behind) and fly down, too. Add one of Dominic's nephews to the mix, and we were a party of twelve.

Now I was *ecstatic!* For the first time in many years, I was going to celebrate my birthday with both family and friends. I was going to pay for a lot of it, but I didn't care. This was a dream come true. Many of my past birthdays had been celebrated with just a few people, wherever I was living or working at the time. I had not celebrated a birthday with family since my wedding thirty years earlier. This was to be a blessed time when I could be not only the center of attention, which God knows I love, but also feel the love of my siblings, nieces, nephews, and special people in my life.

But then, on March 20th, 2020, it happened. COVID-19! The world slammed on its brakes and ground to a halt.

The suddenness of the shutdown was shattering. One day, Las Vegas was its usual city of lights, The Strip dazzling with its marquees advertising A-list performers and its streets teeming with tourists of all ages, colors, and ethnicities. Overnight, The Strip became deserted as all the casinos were closed and locked up. The neon went out. Driving down Las Vegas Boulevard was like passing through a ghostly, deserted playground in some kind of dystopian future.

At first, everyone said, "Don't worry. It will all be over by May." But, of course, it wasn't, and what was worse, we didn't know when or if it would be. When you are in the middle of something this traumatic, not knowing the end date can be terrifying.

My birthday became insignificant in the grand scheme of things and quite *un*spectacular. But it seems I turned eighty anyway. My friend Ruth had me and a couple of others over for meatloaf and cake. For gifts, I received toilet paper and the hard-to-find Clorox wipes!

At the University, we were also in response mode to these new COVID realities. The UNLV campus was, of course, completely closed, but within a week, the Film Department had made an immediate pivot, realizing that it would lose access to all the film students who were in the mid-spring semester. Professor Menendez and others worked night and day to figure out how to teach film directing, acting, cinematography, and costume design without access to camera equipment and each other, a not-so-easy feat!

Very humorous but valuable gifts.

We conducted a crash course in Zoom and devised a way to hold production meetings on Zoom, with each department presenting its research and prep work. Professor Menendez also figured out how each acting student could participate on Zoom from their own homes, with a background projected behind them, and act their parts to the other actor in *their* home, aligning their eye lines so they looked like they were talking to each other. It was far from ideal, but it worked. Teaching continued.

During those early months, we were all wearing masks, not socializing, and staying home. In one way, it wasn't too bad for me, as I was spending a lot of time finishing up my first book, "Stars In Their Underwear." I got a few months of uninterrupted time to approve the cover design and obtain licenses and permissions for the photos. I had been working on it solidly for two years, and now it was time to present my life's stories to the public.

I was both nervous and excited. Nervous because, of course, I wanted everyone to love it, and I was fearful that the people closest to me (my family) might not like or approve of it. But with my parents long gone, I didn't have to worry that they would disagree with my version of events, or drop hints that they didn't like my revealing private matters about the more difficult periods of my young life. I could just envision those raised eyebrows!

It was incredibly exciting when the first actual hard copy of the book arrived at my house, and I could hold it and flip through the pages. After all, this was my life! My story, and my stories. My legacy, in a way, and one I wanted to share.

My books have arrived!

I was so grateful to my mother for saving all my letters home from my early days living on my own, which chronicled in incredible detail the events of my time dancing in *My Fair Lady* and performing on Broadway. I was able to lift entire conversations from those letters and have me speak in my 22-year-old voice as I described the giant Broadway figures of the time—director George Abbott, Stephen Sondheim, Judy Holliday, Bob Fosse, Carol Burnett, Zero Mostel, Barbara Streisand, and so many more. Those letters provided me with details I could never have remembered and gave a true glimpse of New York in the 1960s.

On June 19th, the book was published! It saw some good sales, as all my friends had promised to wait until the copies were available to buy their own. In the following few months, I appeared on several podcasts and one video interview on Channel 8 News. However, I was hindered in promoting the book by COVID-19 restrictions, as I was unable to attend any of the usual book signings at bookstores.

Bit by bit, things opened up, first the "essential" services (nail salons, really?) and restaurants, with specific limitations, and by fall, the first vaccine became available. Getting that first appointment for it was a challenge, as I tried to book one online. Nothing available. Repeatedly, I got that response. Finally, my ancient age of eighty was of some value as I was in the "most at risk" category, being over sixty-five. I finally got my appointment.

On the day, I arrived at Cashman's Center to find a line that stretched for many blocks. I took my place and, after an hour, had moved up, inch by inch, as far as the entrance of the building.

Peeking inside, I expected to be near the front of the line and the military personnel administering the doses. Instead, I saw our line snaking around, back and forth like a bad day at the Miami Airport.

The space was cavernous, industrial, darkish. The floor was cement and hard to stand on. It seemed eerily quiet, other than the occasional announced instructions. It was bizarre and a touch frightening to see only military personnel organizing and directing the proceedings. The six-feet-apart mandate was in full force, so we couldn't even sidle up to the person next in line to chat or exchange the last dire prediction. Those six-foot-apart markings, painted on the floor as large black dots were new to us but soon were to be a common sight. So silently and slowly, we moved from dot to dot, six feet by six feet. It felt like a scene from one of those futuristic movies where everyone is dressed alike in grey jumpsuits, faceless, mindless.

Three hours and one aching back later, I got my vaccination—no ill effects. One step closer, I hoped, to health and normalcy.

One positive thing happened that year because of the COVID-19 pandemic. Rather than my world getting smaller, it got bigger. For this, I thank the internet and the discovery of Zoom.

Zoom became the doorway through which I could seek out and connect with people during this very lonely time. I stumbled upon a website that I hadn't visited in many years, called Journeywoman.com, a travel website based in Toronto. The site was promoting a weekly community call every Friday at 10 a.m. (7 a.m. for me in my time zone). I struggled out of bed early to be awake enough at 7 a.m. and, to my delight, found a community of women, mostly fifty and older, calling in from all over the world - one from Munich who was completely locked down in her apartment, another in Mexico where things were not as strict, others in California and all over the US and Canada. Each week, there would be a subject matter or prompt to get us talking about travel or even how we were just feeling. From this, I bonded with several women and continued to explore the website further.

It is directly from this experience that I submitted my first article to the website, and to my amazement, it got published! It was titled "Life Doesn't End at Eighty, Neither Should Travel"

A couple more articles were published, and soon I was featured as a guest contributor on the subject of "Over 80 Travel!" I hadn't really planned on being the expert in travel for a specific age group, but this was the niche I was assigned, and I ran with it. I have since had over forty articles published. None of this would have happened without COVID-19, Zoom, and the internet.

I also used Zoom to connect with new circles of potential friends, including writers, travelers, dancers, and costume designers, and to explore communities to join. I found my circle of acquaintances enlarging exponentially. I even Zoomed in with a couple of friends who lived in Manchester, England, whom Dominic and I met in 2014 in Sicily. They had been completely housebound for months.

I attended my *first-ever* college reunion via Zoom. Of course, I didn't recognize anyone as they had all grown so damned old!

During the COVID-19 pandemic, the internet saved my sanity and provided connections I wouldn't have otherwise discovered. We all crave connection - it keeps the wolf of loneliness from the door.

JourneyWoman

Solo Travel Over 80: Life Doesn't End at 80 – Neither Should Travel

by Diana Eden | Sep 16, 2020

My first article published in Journeywoman.com

I am sad when I see some of my contemporaries shun the computer. Perhaps they may not have grown up with it as today's young people do, but it is a gift, an asset, a connector, an instructor, and so much more. I entreat those who are still reticent not to put up such a wall of resistance. It can open up your world, just as it did mine.

What an amazing gift to have at our fingertips, every ounce of information we could ever want about any subject we could ever dream up. What fun to have YouTube how-to videos on everything you can imagine, like how to *undo* daisy chain stitches. We can read books, watch movies, and research people, places, and things, and never run out of material.

And the dreaded and ever-scorned social media. "I don't have time," say some people. Others believe it will confer on them all the negative effects it has had on our teenagers and young folk. But if you just want to connect and diminish the feeling of isolation, I am a big fan, especially of Facebook. The young folk complain that it has been taken over by grandmothers sharing photos of their grandkids! And there may be an element of truth to that, but who cares? We are entitled.

Through Facebook, I rekindled friendships with past Broadway friends and castmates, my former costume design colleagues, dancers over forty years old (or fifty or eighty, in my case), UNLV grads, people Dominic and I met on our travels, and fellow writers. It's never too late to reconnect with a long-lost friend or colleague.

Facebook also gives us Oldsters a chance to post old photos of ourselves when we were young, unwrinkled, limber, and in our professional heights. Come on, we've all done it. There's Throwback Thursday, where you post a photo of yourself from the past, and then everyone comments "Gorgeous," "Beautiful," "Amazing," and we all feel very proud of ourselves. And why not? It's fun, and it's harmless.

Having survived my first year as an eighty-year-old in the year of COVID-19, I shifted my long-term sights --is it possible I can actually hit ninety??? Well then, I REALLY want the marching band and the fireworks.

CHAPTER 21
Two Stars and Three Broadway Shows

COVID-19 was still running its course, but in the spring semester, we were allowed to return to campus, but with many restrictions. Students had to sit at desks six feet apart, and we, as teachers, were given an official packet of Clorox wipes, which we had to use to wipe down the doors, handles, and desks before students arrived and after class. It was a strange time indeed.

As we began to emerge from it in April, one of the first events UNLV was able to plan was its annual Hall of Fame Awards. The nominating committee had selected Ann-Margret as the featured recipient due to her many years as a top headliner in Las Vegas and also because the famous dance scene with Elvis in her film *Viva Las Vegas* had been filmed at the old UNLV gym, right in the heart of campus. Knowing my history of working with her, they asked if I could contact her to see if she would accept.

I said yes without hesitation but then struggled mightily to get up the courage to call her. It had been probably thirty-five years since I had seen her, and I no longer had a direct line to the house. A few emails to one of her dancers solved the problem (he checked with her first). Now I had her home phone number. All I had to do was gather the courage to pick up the phone!

It took me *days*. I never liked the phone much anyway, and still being shy (ridiculous at my age), I used an old exercise I was taught during some earlier career coaching. I had to switch the focus to the *other* person and imagine why they would *like* to hear from me. Of course, who wouldn't want to be offered a lovely award?

I eventually made the call. "Hi Ann-Margret, I'm calling because the UNLV Hall of Fame committee has asked me to ask you if you would accept their award this spring, and come in person?" She said yes right away. Hearing her husky voice and little giggle immediately took me back to that first day I met her so many years ago. In 1974, her stage manager drove me up to the house in Benedict Canyon to meet her. I remember it was about 10 a.m. as we were ushered into the lovely, pastel-colored living room. She was still asleep. Shortly afterward, she came out in her bathrobe, hair all tussled, no makeup, and gave me a big welcoming hug as the newest member of her team.

As she hugged me, I was astounded at how tiny she felt! After seeing her on film bursting out in song and dance in *Bye Bye Birdie*, I had expected her to be more solid somehow. In reality, she was petite, like a small bird.

That first meeting marked the beginning of an almost ten-year relationship that involved traveling with her and her company to Las Vegas (who knew at the time it would eventually become my home) and Lake Tahoe, outfitting her dancers and singers and eventually designing for the star herself. I became one of the Ann-Margret family, as indeed, she bonded closely with all who worked for her. She is still close with many of her former dancers and sees some of them regularly.

But now, fifty years later, I had to call her a second time and find out how the university should reach her and make the necessary arrangements. I didn't want to give out her home number.

I couldn't wait to see her. Would I be able to tell her how much she had meant to me in the early days of my costume career? How much I admired her and even wanted to dance and sing like her? In fact, how working with her was the springboard which launched my own career into costume design?

At the Hall of Fame event, I was seated at a small table at the front with her and her manager. She gave me a big welcoming hug and we had a few quick words. In due course, I was called up to the stage to introduce her with a few congratulatory words. My heart was beating wildly, and I prayed that I wouldn't forget the speech I had written. After she accepted the Hall of Fame Award, there were crowds around her, fans and VIPS all wanting a moment of her time and a photograph with her. And before I knew it, she was gone. So much for catching up!

Another event made the highlight reel of 2021 -- my first and only book signing at a store called "Just Fabulous" in Palm Springs. Since most of their book signings were by major celebrities or well-known authors, I suspected I got mine in return for putting the owner in touch with Bob Mackie's people. But who cared? Bob had a major new publication about to release.

A happy reunion with Ann-Margret, Hall of Fame Awards, UNLV, April 2022

I made the pilgrimage with my good friend Ruth, where we combined a week's stay in her time-share and visiting her cousins with promoting the book signing event by asking stores to display the posters in their windows wherever we could.

The Saturday of my event finally came, and I was a nervous wreck. But bless his heart, Bob Mackie did indeed come *and* bought one of my books! He is a star in his own right, one of the greatest costume designers of our time, but still has remained kind and generous. I worried if he would be curious enough to actually read my book and learn about my descriptions of his place, Elizabeth Courtney Costumes, and of my replacing his dress for Ann-Margret with one of my own designs. (I always felt guilty for that.)

I still don't know if he read it.

*My mentor Bob Mackie and I at the
Just Fabulous bookstore in Palm Springs, Ca.*

The world continued to emerge slowly from the effects of the pandemic. In September, I saw that the Broadway theaters were finally reopening their doors after having been shuttered for eighteen long months during COVID. Feeling nostalgic about my old Broadway days, I decided I must go and support the shows' re-openings. Before caution could change my mind, I booked the flights and chose three shows I wanted to see. The theaters were just opening their box offices, so good seats were still available.

Traveling to New York was like going on a roller coaster ride. From my quiet suburban desert home in Las Vegas, Times Square came on like a heavy-metal rock concert. Looking out my 30th-floor window in the Marriott Marquis Hotel, hearing the constant noise of honking cabs and fire engine sirens, and seeing the brilliant colors of giant video screens all competing for attention, provided me with sensory overload.

No longer the 22-year-old I was when I lived in New York in a fourth-floor walk-up apartment and danced at night on the Broadway stages, I took my whirlwind three-day New York visit in small bites, with oases of quiet in between the highlights. Since I had booked the hotel right on Times Square, it had the advantage of being a few short blocks from all the theaters and restaurants. And close enough for me to duck back to my room for quick naps.

On the first day, I met up with my dear friend and producer, Ethan Walker, and we headed to the Showstoppers Costume Exhibit on 42nd Street. It proved to be one of the best I've ever seen. During COVID, the costume houses that create the incredible clothes that we see on the Broadway stages were suddenly shuttered, with no way to pay enormous New York rents or skilled artisans. Banding together, they formed the Costume Industry Coalition Recovery Fund, and this exhibit was one of the beautiful products that emerged to raise money for their industry.

I was dazzled. Though a costume designer myself, I still can get goosebumps from seeing the extraordinary skill and originality that these world-class costumes present. I feel immensely proud to be part of the costume industry.

Walking back up 8th Avenue, Ethan and I stopped by one of the theaters where I performed in 1963, when it was The Alvin Theater, now called the Neil Simon Theater. A new show was loading in with large black boxes of equipment spilling out onto the sidewalk, but the house manager, Judy Brown, was interested enough in my history with the theater to give us a private tour. The interior has been thoroughly renovated, and the giant chandelier has been lowered and cleaned to sparkling perfection. What a joy it was to stand on the balcony, looking at *the exact spot* on stage where I had once danced in *A Funny Thing Happened on the Way to the Forum*. I am also immensely proud to be part of the Broadway community.

Reliving my past glory in the balcony of the Neil Simon Theater

Dinner was at Joe Allen's Restaurant, beloved of all theatergoers for nearly sixty years. I happened to be one of its early customers in its original location on the East Side (I was dating the bartender) before its current location on West 46th Street opened in 1963. It looked just the same as I remember it, with its brick arches and show posters on the walls.

On the second day of my whirlwind weekend, I visited the 9/11 Memorial and Museum at the south end of Manhattan. There, I found the two memorial pools that are in the footprints of the Twin Towers. All I hear is the soft sound of water running down the four walls and disappearing into the blackness at the center. Voices are hushed or silenced. It is a somber and reflective place, and the only colors that stay in my mind are grey, black, and the white of a rose left in tribute to somebody's loved one

In the cab coming back, I travel up West Street, where once fire engines raced down to the towers. Now, I witness local New Yorkers walking their dogs and jogging or bicycling along the path adjacent to the river. The sun shines brightly, and life feels normal and good.

Two other shows round out my crazy weekend.

One is *Waitress*, written by and starring Sara Bareilles. The audience was so happy to be back in the theater that they applauded before the show started as the lights dimmed, as if to say, "We are here for you and so very grateful you are back." I left the theater just feeling joy about life, about people, about the ability to go to the theater.

Producer and dear friend Ethan Walker and I
about to attend "Waitress"

My weekend ended with a big bang -- the exuberant musical concert *SIX*, with Henry VIII's six wives dressed in glittery punk versions of Tudor splendor.

So, two days, three shows, one museum, one exhibition, one unexpected private tour, it's a lot for an eighty-one-year-old, but I made it! Nostalgia and adrenaline got me through it, and once home, I was able to collapse for a day before I taught my next class at UNLV. Never a dull moment.

CHAPTER 22
The Call of the Wild

At eighty-two, I was beginning to really understand that opportunities and time to do things I had always wanted to do were running short, or at least shorter. It's easy to think that one has an indefinite time, but in one's eighties, reality starts to tell a different tale. When the news announces the death of someone famous, I now check how old they were.

One thing I always wanted to do was visit Africa and go on a safari to see the wild animals. I thought about it for years but never really made concrete plans, largely because of the expense and the distance. But it was getting to be now or never.

I signed up for a sixteen-day trip with a friend, who, shortly after, dropped out. Undaunted, I continued planning as once there, we were to join a tour presented by Overseas Adventure Travel. I knew there were to be about fourteen people on the trip, and I figured, "Not *all* of them will be idiots." In other words, being with fourteen strangers couldn't be all that bad.

But at eighty-two, I knew my stamina would not allow me to do the whole plane itinerary in one fell swoop. I have long been a proponent in my travel articles of breaking up a long trip by staying somewhere halfway at an airport hotel. But the distance to South Africa was so far that I took *three* days to get there. Day one, Las Vegas to New York. Day two, a fourteen-hour (yes, fourteen!) flight to Dubai, and day three, an eleven-hour flight to Johannesburg. The good news is that I was relatively fresh when I arrived, compared to the basket case I could have been if I'd done the thirty-three hours without a break. I also splurged for business class for the first time in my life, and it was glorious!

I have discovered, as I have traveled and write about the challenges of traveling as an older person, that the most difficult part of a trip is *getting there* (and getting back). The worst part of any vacation, especially one going outside of the US or Canada, is surviving the airport experience.

Airports are not old-age-friendly, that is for certain. One needs stamina, patience, and the physique of a marathon runner to get from your drop-off to your departure gate, which often is over a mile from the starting point. Lines form first at the check-in counters, especially during peak travel times. Standing is tough for me.

Then you head for the TSA security checkpoint. You must remove jackets, belts, and jewelry and other miscellaneous articles of clothing. Once through, clutching your boarding pass, jacket, belt, and phone, you pick up your carryon and hop to an area where you can reassemble, trying not to get flustered by the rush of people right behind you. At least we can now keep our shoes on. When was the last time a senior snuck a forbidden object through in her orthotic Dr. Comforts?

And next is a long walk to your gate, which of course is always the one at the farthest end of the concourse. And by now, your carry-on luggage is feeling heavier by the minute.

For gates and transfers that I already know are long walks (up to a mile or more), I book a wheelchair. At first, I had to fight the guilt that I didn't deserve it, not being handicapped with anything other than age-related shortness of breath and lack of stamina. In fact, disapproving stares have sometimes been thrown at me at the gate when I leap up like a spring chicken to walk down the gangway to the plane's entrance. (You'd think I had just elbowed multiple one-legged elders out of the way to get my ride.)

What works for me, besides chanting "everything will be beautiful when I get there" over and over, is to give myself as much self-care as possible en route. I have my favorite blow-up cushion to ease the meeting of back versus seat, warm socks, earplugs, an eye mask, and a couple of Tylenol PMs. I have been known to have a cocktail, though all my sources tell me this is *not* good to do on a long flight.

But back to Africa. It turned out to be a magnificent experience. I only once felt *alone* when at our first camp, the various groups of friends, families and couples were posing for photos together with the magnificent expanse of Africa behind them. Trying not to sound like "poor me," I asked someone to take a photo of me solo, same Africa behind me. I really missed being part of a group.

As far as being a suitable trip for me as an eighty-three-year-old, nothing was too much of a challenge. We rode in jeeps that were quite comfy, and there was no hiking or long-distance walking. One did need to be able to squat, though, on the three-hour game drives as we went behind what is referred to as "the green door," i.e., a bush, to take care of business when no Ladies' Rooms were available! I also took frequent short naps whenever I could in between excursions, and early bedtime in the bush was not a problem, as once the sun went down, there was nothing much to do. Our guides always escorted us back to our cabins to make sure an errant lion or elephant wasn't lingering in the area. (We could hear the sounds of them at night, though, which was exotic and quite thrilling.)

Happy in Africa, but wishing I were part of a couple,
or a trio of friends

In our first camp in Botswana, we saw few animals (one lovely elephant family at a pool, and a solo giraffe somewhat at a distance), and I was wondering if the posters had all been lying. I don't count guinea fowl as African Big Five. I confess I was impatient and a bit worried. Had I been fooled by the travel posters and social media reels showing an abundance of lions surrounded by adorable cubs?

Our next camp in Zambia was on a river, and we saw plenty of hippos. My tent cabin was beside the path where they exited at night from the river to feed inland and then re-enter at dawn. Being a sound sleeper, I missed that sight. However, there were plenty of silly monkeys having fun on my roof the next morning. I was careful not to leave laundered underwear on the railings, as apparently, they love to steal it. I didn't want to see my underpants on the head of some primate!

It was here that I had one of the most magical experiences of my life. We were at breakfast and were called to jump in the jeeps quickly, as a leopard had been sighted. We drove fast to the area and crashed through a lot of deep, bumpy brush before we paused.

"Look!" cried someone.

"Where? Where?" I replied, looking frantically and seeing nothing but tall yellow brush. And then, as if by pure magic, the magnificent leopard emerged, just his head, and then more of him. He looked around and then, just as magically, he vanished before our eyes. He emerged again, and I got to film his beautiful slow walk, and then his climb up into a tree to enjoy his recent kill—it was an impala for lunch today.

We moved to our third camp in Botswana, where I experienced even more awe-inspiring moments, every bit worth the three days it took to get to Africa. One evening at sunset, we descended into the valley next to the river and saw giraffes, spreading their front legs to either side (no bending at the knee, I am told) to drink from the water, their reflection presenting a gorgeous double image. Then out of the bush came a family of elephants who walked down to the river and crossed it to the pasture on the other side. Then more elephants emerge. And more. And then more, like clowns from a Volkswagen. Until there were nearly 80 or 90 elephants in family groups, matriarchs with "kids" of diminishing sizes, traveling down to the river. "Kids" stopped to splash in the water, mothers gave them a nudge and a reprimand to keep going. They paraded by, blissfully unaware of us as we sat in our jeeps not far away. As the sun set, they grazed peacefully on the other side of the river.

What a magnificent creature looking back at me

Oh, to be an animal without knowledge of politics, or aging, or of financial worries, or lost friends. To live among zebras, giraffes, pelicans, and so many more in complete peace. Or at least for that moment. Perhaps it is over-romanticized to think their lives have no stress, but on this evening, it seemed like all was well on our planet Earth.

These experiences live vividly in my mind and remain examples of the true reason for travel, to see things that stir the heart and soul, and to feel a sense of awe.

CHAPTER 23
The Holiday Blues

OK, let's face it, it's considered "whiney" to complain too loudly about how much the holidays suck for a single and childless person during the Christmas season. But it is a time when being alone really feels acute. No parents, no kids, no husband. Boo-hoo me.

The thing is that the Christmas/New Year holidays (unlike Thanksgiving, which I love) are three to four weeks long. During this time, I am constantly reminded of family groupings and bombarded with good cheer, kids, merry this, happy that… when mostly, I feel a sense of deep loneliness. It doesn't help that Dominic is gone, nor that the days are short, dark, and cold.

Families can be blood or chosen, but you don't *really* feel alone until all your single friends are unavailable to join you because they are with their own offspring. My adopted family of friends and co-workers all have children and grandchildren, it seems, all but a very few.

Part of the problem is that my usual schedule is interrupted. Regularly scheduled events are suspended. Normality, structure, and social contacts are missing. My yoga class, where we all share brief introductory stories before we start working the muscles, is suspended until January. My crafting group, which I go to weekly, more for company and conversation than sewing, is similarly on hiatus. The university where I teach is closed for the four-week Christmas break. Even my clubhouse and gym are closed for a few days during the festivities. I miss the structure.

But I am lucky to have vivid memories of the holidays with my family growing up, a long time ago.

These memories are less triggered by the sense of smell (turkeys roasting, cookies baking) than by one particular sense of touch. As kids in England, we went to bed on Christmas night, knowing there would be a Christmas stocking for each of us from Father Christmas in the morning on our bed. How exciting to wake up and feel this heavy lump at the foot of the bed. I can feel its weight now!

At seven a.m., we were invited to get in bed with Mum and Dad to open our stockings. There was always an orange in the toe of the stocking and a few walnuts, for some reason, plus a few little silly gifts - puzzles, a chocolate bar, and so forth. This was really fun, and we were all together. It was cozy and warm in every sense of the word.

Another Christmas memory I have is of our dad sitting in the big armchair in the living room with a large wooden board on his lap. To this board were attached (with pushpins) pieces of paper, one for each of us, on which he would write what each newly-opened gift was and from whom it came. We could only unwrap the next one once the information was duly noted. This was so that later we could have an accurate list of whom to write thank you notes to. How terribly British!

Later in Canada, I remember the sumptuous Christmas dinner of turkey, ham, and trimmings. I remember little about the cooking of it, but the presentation was everything. Mum would have laid out her best white damask tablecloth, on which rested the best china with its gold leaf decoration. Richly ornate casserole dishes had been polished to perfection and contained the vegetables, and a silver gravy boat on its own saucer held the luscious brown liquid. Cut crystal wine and water glasses made the table sparkle. I remember a small silver rectangular dish on four legs with a dark blue glass insert that held the salt and a tiny silver spoon.

Contrary to today's wishes to be comfortable, this was always an occasion where we dressed up. I loved that. Party dresses for my sister and me, my brother looking sharp, Mum in a beautiful 1950s cocktail dress, and Dad in his best suit and tie. Dressing up made the event feel like a real occasion, an event of import, a special celebration. Those were during my teenage years until I left home at age twenty-one, and only occasionally was I able to make it home for the holiday feast from wherever I was living or performing.

My first Christmas away from home was in Pittsburgh, where I was performing in *My Fair Lady* at the Shubert Theater in 1961. My friend and fellow dancer, Elinor, and I were roommates, and a few days before Christmas, we went out and bought a real Christmas tree, about six feet tall, and then snuck it up the back elevator of our hotel and into our room. We moved the beds around so they were more like settees against the wall. We decorated the tree with popcorn and the ribbon bows from our small gifts as we unwrapped them. I am sure the housekeeping staff were not one bit amused!

Another Christmas, I was in rehearsal in Los Angeles for the National Company of *The Odd Couple*. We were to open a few days after Christmas at the James Doolittle Theater on Vine Street. Some of us wanted to celebrate with dinner and ended up at a Chinese restaurant on Hollywood Boulevard, the only place that was open on Christmas Day. That group included one of the stars, Richard Benjamin, his wife Paula Prentiss, Peter Boyle (later to become famous in the *Everybody Loves Raymond* TV series), and a few other cast members. We had a great time eating our sweet and sour chicken Christmas dinner, and we laughed non-stop.

For many Christmases, though, before Dominic, I found myself living alone, first in New York and then in Los Angeles, hoping that I would be invited somewhere for Christmas Day.

Dominic loved Christmas, the family events (with his large Italian family), cooking, visiting, and playing games. Every other year, we traveled to Buffalo, New York, to be with his family, where he was in his element, reminiscing and making everyone laugh. I suffered a bit during those marathon family gatherings, where they all sat around a table, drank wine, and shared stories… *for eight to ten hours* at a time! As an introvert, I have a shelf life of about four hours, tops. But bless them, Dominic's family eventually got used to me tiptoeing up to bed when the party was still in full swing.

My family was Canadian, more formal, and usually sent hand-written invitations saying, "Do Come for Cocktails and Caroling, 7 to 9 p.m." Dominic was truly horrified at the idea of putting an end time on an invitation.

At our own home in Los Angeles, we used to put up a tree and then leave for our Christmas visit, returning just in time to take it down. As the childless ones, we were assigned the role of the visitors, which felt like it minimized our own valid need to be home for the holidays. We were the untethered ones. Being the "defectors" is the price of having set out at a young age for parts unknown, for careers and adventure, leaving the security and comfort of a larger family behind.

Then in 2023, I met a lovely woman in Toronto who expressed similar feelings about the holidays, and finally, I realized that it was okay to feel this way. I was not alone. She told me she had booked a trip to Morocco right over Christmas to distract her from the empty feelings. Sounded like a great idea. A few days later, I found myself saying,

"Maybe I could go too!" I called her and she said, "Of course, please join me," so I signed up.

It was just what I needed. I joined a group of twelve, mostly in their forties, all singles, all avoiding the holidays in one way or another. We traveled by van (not a terribly fancy one) from Casablanca to Fez, and then to the Sahara Desert and back, staying in riads, tents, and hotels. We had fabulous local experiences, especially as they related to cooking and food. I got to practice putting wood on an ancient wood-burning stove, kneading dough to make bread, and watching local women peel and dice vegetables faster than I could ever imagine possible. And this is me, a non-cook!

But mostly we got to laugh. Sometimes it was at the most unexpected and ridiculous moments.

On the night we stayed overnight in the Sahara Desert, we were in tents situated right on the sand. It was bitterly cold, and I lay in bed wondering if I would ever be warm again. In the middle of the night, I needed to visit the toilet, which was in a building at the far end of the camp, so I threw on my coat and ran in my bare feet at full speed in its direction. Halfway, I had to stop to catch my breath, and clutching my coat around me, I looked up to see the most amazing stars I had ever seen in my life! I had never seen stars so bright, or seemingly close and so abundant. I was shivering and hopping up and down, but totally in awe.

On Christmas Day, we were in Chefchaouen, "the blue city," and were escorted by our guide on a walking and shopping tour of the old quarter. Then we were left to our own devices for a couple of hours, and I found myself sitting on a terrace sipping coffee, overlooking the kasbah and central square of this lovely town. I was entirely content and cared not a whit that it was December 25th.

However, one event on that trip brought me face-to-face with the perils of my "advanced" age. I was reminded that falls are one of the biggest dangers in getting older, leading to all sorts of broken or strained bits and pieces.

Exiting a magnificent, tiled four-story restaurant, Restaurant Nejjarine, into the dark medieval passageway of the medina in Fez at night, I was looking for my glasses in my purse so I could see the way better. But, silly me, I failed to halt while I completed the search. Still walking, I was reaching for them when my foot hit an uneven paver and I went down hard, with no arms to break the fall. I landed on my face. Full splat. As I went down, I thought," Oh-oh, this is it. This is the fall

144

we all dread. The fall that requires us to get airlifted back to the US. The fall that ends travel as we know it. My life might as well be over."

Overlooking the kasbah and the square on December 25th, 2022

The feel of the impact, face onto stone, was brutal. I did not pass out but was stunned. One of the women in the group came round in front of me and got me sitting up. "Look at me," she said, making eye contact, "I've got you. Breathe slowly, another breath, slowly, slowly." She was such a calming angel. Ice arrived. My cheek hurt like hell. I was afraid I had broken my cheekbone, perhaps even the entire side of my face.

A weird silence surrounded me as the rest of our group looked on anxiously.

"Well, this was certainly a buzz kill. Sorry, everyone!" I chirped as cheerfully as I could. Our poor tour leader, I thought, is probably thinking, "There's always some old fart who does this. And now I'm going to have to take her to the ER and fill out paperwork."

As it turned out, nothing was broken, although I sported a very black eye for a few days. But I decided, black eye be damned, I would continue the tradition of taking a trip somewhere over the holidays in the years to come.

Me, pretending I don't have a big black eye!

CHAPTER 24
AGE 83: A Kick-Ass Woman!

In the spring of my 83rd birthday, I was feeling on top of the world. "Wow," I thought to myself, "this is really just fine. I feel well, and opportunities both social and professional are still coming my way. I still have value out in the world."

I had been awarded an honor named "Woman of Achievement" by the Nevada Women's Film Festival which made me feel wonderful. I was just so sad that Dominic was not alive to witness me receiving this and see the incredible tribute reel that a number of people, including Professor Menendez and some of my clients, had put together for me.

Nothing feels better than being recognized by one's colleagues

In March, I was flown to New York to appear on a travel panel for Journeywoman called "Kick-Ass Women Over Fifty" at the annual

Women's Travel Fest. And indeed, I felt like a Kick-Ass Woman! I was put up in a hotel in Soho with a view of the Brooklyn Bridge and walked the three blocks to the location of the two-day event.

In the morning, we heard several presentations on travel, and then in the afternoon, our panel was up. I was seated on stage, next to Carolyn Ray (the interviewer and CEO of Journeywoman), and two other travel experts, and we answered questions about traveling as older women. I had been dared by my niece Amelia to use a line I had said to her earlier in private—that as an older traveler, I found there were "more naps, less orgasms".

Could I really say that? Could I get away with it? I actually *did* say it, and there was a gasp of shock and then a wave of laughter that went on for a full minute. "I can't believe you just said that," my fellow panelist Dawn said. But it got their attention. You want a "kickass woman over fifty" panelist? You got one!

Getting a big laugh on the panel at the Womens' Travel Fest,
with CEO Carolyn Ray, Dawn Booker

I attended all the presentations on Day Two but skipped the closing night party—the avoidance of crowds, noise, and too much alcohol is one of the nods I give to my aging persona. Back to my nice hotel room, tucked in bed early, ready to fly home the next day and be ready to teach again at UNLV the day after.

A month later, I fulfilled a long-held dream to visit Bora Bora, where I got to swim with the manta rays. Our guide was a deeply tanned and fit Frenchman, around sixty, with grey hair in a ponytail, a bit of a "hippy" in appearance. He took one look at me, this slow-moving, eighty-something-year-old in a bathing suit amidst his other young and fit thirty-year-old snorkelers and rolled his eyes. Well, his back was to me, but I swear he rolled his eyes. He did have to tow me from the boat to the area where the manta rays were, as I didn't think I could swim that far. What an extraordinary sight they were—three of them—gliding through the water so close to me! It was hypnotizing and I was quite proud of myself.

In fact, I was feeling pretty proud of myself that whole spring. The only symptom, if you will, of my deteriorating body was that I got very out of breath when climbing stairs (even a few) or going uphill on a hike. So, I decided to sign up for personal training for a month at the Y.

I was assigned a trainer, let's call him Don, who was in his seventies, an army veteran, who limped a bit, and was in his last days of training people prior to getting a knee replacement. He put me through my paces on the circuit of machines for upper and lower body strength, and I thought he was being far too tame with me. I wanted to add more weights and feel like I was getting my money's worth.

"I've never seen anyone your age in this good condition," he would tell me. At first, I was pleased, but then he told me the same thing every session I had (twice a week) until it got to be a bit annoying. I realized he was probably saying it to all his clients. And yet he was still very conservative with my weights and repetitions.

Well, pride comes before a fall, I guess. A month after I finished my month's program, I woke up one morning and as I tried to get up, I suddenly felt shooting pains down the back of both legs, so acute I was gasping. It hurt like hell to move at all, but gradually, I maneuvered myself inch by inch over the bed until my feet touched the floor, and then inch by inch straightened up.

Though I have had scoliosis since my forties (and maybe before, I can't actually remember) and have had moderate back pain when in situations where I have had to sit a long time, like on a plane, it's never seemed to be very acute or interfere with my life in any major way.

But this was different. It did not go away. And I attribute this very moment to when I actually started to feel "old" for the first time. Every morning, I go through the same agonizing torture to get out of bed and hobble to the bathroom. The toilet seat seems to have sunk two inches lower than I remember it. I hobble back and then have the agony of the underpants - how to reach down to get my foot in the hole and then the other one and get the damn pants pulled up. Yes, the word "hobble" has entered my vocabulary. Also, "stooped".

Weeks went by. I went to the doctor. She ordered X-rays (nothing bad apparently) and requested I do six weeks of physical therapy. But it didn't help.

I confess I have not been very tolerant of people with chronic pain in the past (except for my sister's pain, which is constant, varied, and massive). People my age and younger complained of "bad backs" and said they could no longer travel because of bad hips or bad knees, and I wasn't the most sympathetic. Though I would never accept that I *really* thought this way, in the back of my mind I was thinking, "Well, if they just tried harder." Forgive me, folks. I sincerely apologize.

What my continuing daily pain has done is really make me confront getting old. I honestly thought my joints would keep well-oiled and working fine forever. This has been a wake-up call, and I can't say I am too happy about it. When I do my hobble to the bathroom each morning, stooped over and saying bad words, I really feel for the first time that my body is deteriorating. Until I felt daily pain (and I grant it is mild compared to some), and faced the fact that this is "parts wearing out" or "parts rubbing against other parts where once there was cushioning," did I realize it might be a permanent situation for the rest of my days. If only there were a WD-40 for the joints.

My doctor almost shrugged when X-rays showed my back pain came mostly from arthritis, and he advised me to take Tylenol. The old "take two aspirins and call me in the morning." On the other hand, I don't really want him recommending tons of painkillers or suggesting surgery either. Damned if you do, damned if you don't.

The other thing that happened is that I stopped worrying about what we, as older people, are called. Call me old, I don't care. I describe myself as such to my students at UNLV all the time, and it doesn't bother me.

As in "I'm sorry, I don't know who (insert big pop star name here) is, but I'm old. Do you know who Nina Simone was?"

Much has been written recently in articles delving into the culture's treatment of old people (there, I said it), and how they feel diminished, ignored, slandered, and invisible. Being called elderly has not gone over well, though being an "elder" does have the ring of wisdom, as in "the Village Elders". We've been called "seasoned," no, not with salt and pepper. I don't think Golden Ager is a good description, considering all the shit that may be coming our way, and senior is okay, though it reminds me of school.

I even had some business cards made for the Women's Travel Fest, toting myself as a "Vintage Traveler," perhaps like a fine wine. In fact, this led to confusion. People thought I traveled to street fairs in search of vintage items, not that *I* was vintage!

I very much like the term "oldster" revived and repurposed by author Sari Botton, who created a successful Substack about aging. She says, "I didn't coin the term. 'Oldster'. It is an old word that was a bit of a slur. It was a dismissive way of referring to an elder. I'm turning it into a positive, and using it to describe people of all ages, who are getting older, which is everyone."

So go ahead and call me old, or an oldster. Just don't treat me as feeble, stupid, infirm, out-of-touch, demented, decrepit, or any other such diminishing term... at least until I *am* feeble, stupid, infirm, etc.

CHAPTER 25
PUSHING BOUNDARIES: The Arrival of Humility

Towards the end of 2023, I wanted to push boundaries a bit and see if I was up to a seven-day cruise on a tiny boat (as compared to a massive fourteen-story cruise ship), in fact a catamaran, with four small cabins. Was this suitable for a "vintage traveler" like myself? I wasn't worried about getting seasick, but would getting in and out of a dinghy to get to shore be doable? Would my balance be okay climbing up and down the ladders from deck to deck? Would I miss the luxuries of large bathrooms with little free shampoos? Could I share a double bed with a roommate, not to mention the cabin, which only had an eight-inch walkway around the edge of the bed?

I wasn't sure, but I wanted to try, so I signed up. It was with Captain Joy Sherman, whom I had met at the Women's Travel Fest the previous year.

As it turned out, all my concerns turned out to be for nothing. My roommate turned out to be my sister. I brought my own shampoo. I clung to the railings when moving about the vessel. But I confess, getting off the boat and into a tiny rubber dinghy was a challenge and one that I didn't want to have anyone watch, or take photos to post on Facebook!

To enter the rubber dinghy thing, you first have to sit down on the lip of the back deck of the catamaran. From a standing position, you can bend your knees until you are in an ungainly squat, bottom out, and hope that it will reach the last twelve inches down to the floor. You also run the risk of it NOT going that far down, in which case you fall backwards and your legs go flying up in the air in a most undignified "dead bug" position! Or you can go down onto all fours facing the dinghy, but are then confronted with the complicated maneuver of getting your feet around and in front of you, a near-impossible maneuver except for the classically Cirque-du-Soleil-trained. But by the last day of the cruise, I had the sequence pretty much down.

Other than those graceless moves, the trip was a delight, and entirely doable for a senior traveler.

May came and went, and I turned another year older. How on earth can I be 84 years old? But I must still travel while I can.

I ordered walking sticks for my upcoming trip to Greece. Is it really a cane or a walking stick? If it is a cane, then I have to face the fact that I will look like an old lady with a cane!! Can my pride and vanity handle that?

As it turned out, my vanity was the least of my worries. I fell on the second day of our Greece trip, passing out, and breaking my ankle. What was injured far more than my bone was my pride, my dignity, my confidence, and my self-image as a healthy, adventurous 84-year-old, loving travel, telling my readers on Journeywoman, "You Can Do It! You can do it whether it's climbing up on jeeps on an African Safari, or transferring from a catamaran to a dinghy in the British Virgin Islands." People have called me intrepid and indomitable. I hardly felt that anymore, even though I kept telling myself that what happened to me had nothing whatsoever to do with age and could have happened to anyone..

Carol and I at the highest point in the island of Santorini, Greece

Low clouds over our part of Santorini left some dew on the terrace pavement. When I opened the door of our apartment to our lovely sitting area where we would have breakfast, I slipped and went down hard. I don't even remember falling. The first thing I remember was my sister trying to get me to a sitting position on the bench. "Where am I?" I asked her. "What happened?" Apparently, I asked her this several times and forgot that she had answered me. A bit scary! I could see the lovely white cave-style houses of Oia across the water along the top of the volcanic cliffs, but I couldn't quite put together where we were.

I took a two-hour lie-down and seemed better when I woke up ("Yes, Carol, we are in Santorini, I know now."). My ankle was swollen and painful, but not unbearable. So, intrepid traveler that I was, we set off on a sightseeing tour around the island.

By the next morning, I knew things were worse, and I needed to go to the hospital.

She was at my side the entire time and did most of the reorganizing and rerouting, like the GPS when you miss a turnoff. I wouldn't have made it without her.

But we also depended on "the kindness of strangers". Let me introduce them.

The first was Sotiris, our Santorini villa concierge and driver. Though he managed several properties, when we needed him, he was there in an instant, relaxed in his demeanor and with a big smile on his face. Nothing seemed too much trouble. He put his arm under my shoulder to lift me down the stairs to the car, came into the clinic, introduced us to the Greek nurses at the intake desk, and ensured we were being taken care of. Then he was off to help another client, returning later to take my sister back to the villa and back again the next morning to help get us to the port. Always with a smile and a positive attitude. A beautiful sunshine soul.

The next soul was not only an angel of mercy but, it turned out, a remarkably accomplished orthopedic surgeon who happened to be in Santorini on rotation from Athens. We looked him up online and found that he had reportedly done over 50,000 operations. He told me he travels to the US three to four times a year for meetings, and loves Las Vegas, especially the Texas de Brazil steakhouse. Small world.

I said to him, "I think you may be a fairly famous doctor, right?" He paused a moment and then, with a twinkle in his eye, said, "Maybe."

A helping hand when I needed it.
Photo by Carol Moore-Ede

At the beginning of my operation, the anesthetist was having trouble getting the needle into my spine, which is quite twisted from scoliosis. I was crying out in pain with each new needle attempt. Dr. Papagiannopoulis (my Greek God /surgeon/savior) lifted me in a bear hug and said to me, "Everything will be all right, my love." Never have I welcomed words more. The needle eventually found its mark, my ankle was repaired, and I spent the night in the clinic.

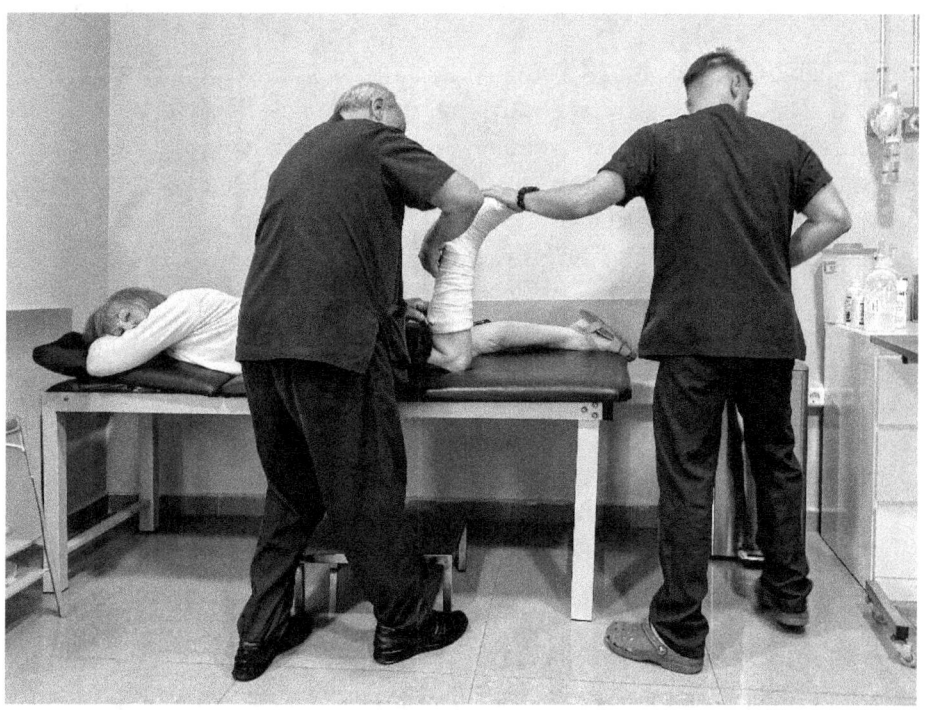

Being attended to by my Greek saviors
Photo by Carol Moore-Ede

In the morning, my doctor had already returned to Athens, but Carol and Sotiris were there to pick up a still stunned and fragile me and get us to the ferry to Crete.

The boarding of our ferry to Crete was like a slapstick comedy! A wheelchair had been ordered for me at the dock, but it never showed up. As the crowds of people suddenly started moving forward and into the jaws of the giant ferry, being absorbed faster than I could imagine, a policeman saw my dilemma and radioed for a chair. Suddenly, a man with a chair at the ferry ran at full speed towards me, threw me in it, so to speak, and ran full tilt toward the giant ramp that led into the mouth of the ferry. By now, whistles and loud horns of all kinds were going off, urgent warning of the raising of the "drawbridge," and I wondered if we would make it or even get caught on it as it was being raised. I couldn't turn around, couldn't see Carol at all. In no time at all, the ramp was up, doors closed, and I was in the dark interior hull. Oh no, I thought, Carol didn't make it. Disaster! Phones were losing juice. Was she left at the port with no way to get back up the cliff? No place to stay? I was sick with anxiety.

Thank God, she finally popped into my field of vision, flustered but present. The paper bag she was carrying had broken, spilling all my medical papers and x-rays, some jars of honey from breakfast, two tiny, hard-boiled eggs, also from breakfast, and my black lace bra. (On getting dressed to leave the clinic, I decided a bra was just too much irritation on my skin, and who in Greece would care anyway if my breasts were saggy.)

We made it to Crete, picked up our car, and headed the one-hour drive to our villa as darkness set in. By now, I was feeling awful, exhausted, in a post-operative fog, upset with myself, and guilty that Carol was going to spend much of her holiday looking after me. We had to cancel a "dinner with a local" experience we had booked, paid for, and were looking forward to.

"Don't tell *anyone* about my accident," I told her, feeling foolish about the whole thing. But she had already posted on Facebook anyway, along with a number of paparazzi-like photos detailing my entire experience at the clinic. I was mortified, and ready to be furious! Yet the comments were all so supportive. "You've got this," friends said, "nothing keeps you down". But I felt they were giving me credit for far more bravery than I deserved.

What no one tells you is that when you have a catastrophic event, the 84-year-old person (me), organizer of trips, university professor, creator of costumes, general problem solver, this person leaves the room. Who is left is a three-year-old sitting on the floor, crying.

The idea of making a plan of action, looking for help, reorganizing flights, and all of that seemed overwhelming. Calling the airline and getting the menu of options, none of which seemed like the right one, waiting endlessly on hold, getting hung up on ("Thank you for your call. Goodbye."), and then starting over again, all this seemed daunting. Then, needing to find one's verification code (sent to your email), booking number, and who knows what else… all this is just a task too much for a three-year-old.

I also lapsed into a short-lived depression, shedding tears, and getting a scary glimpse into that very deep, dark pit I have experienced before in a lifetime of dealing with depression at different times in my life. It's a feeling I don't wish on anyone. It's a physical as well as mental state that takes over your whole persona, a state in which no hope of things getting better seems possible. I believe I actually told my poor sister I wanted to die! And all this while we were staying in a glorious villa on a hill with a 180° view over the north coast of Crete and the sparkling blue Mediterranean Sea.

I felt better the next day, and we were able to enjoy a couple of days of tourism, but my mobility was limited. I posted cheery photos on Facebook of me with a thumbs-up sign.

A brave gesture can't hide my grim face
Photo by Carol Moore-Ede

We had one more river to cross, though. Aegean Airlines refused to issue me a boarding pass for my upcoming flight back to Athens to start the long flights home, telling me I needed a signed form stating I was "fit to fly". With the help of our villa host, we got one from the local MD in the nearby town and thought that was that. But no, *not good enough*. They needed the form signed by the surgeon who had performed my operation, who was by now back in Athens.

I felt this dread, that I was never going to get home, that I would be stranded so far away at the mercy of red tape, that there was no one to sort it out or advocate for me, that I would end up in a fetal position under a rock.

But there was a good ending. Again, our Greek host at the villa was able to reach my surgeon on his cell phone on a Saturday night, no less, and get the paperwork accomplished.

I had more lessons to learn. One was what it is like to be wheelchair dependent. I am grateful for the many wheelchair agents who pushed me from point to point, but the experience can make you feel helpless. My Aegean Airlines plane did not have a jetway, only a steep set of metal stairs up to the plane entrance. I had to be hoisted up in a lift, sort of like a cherry picker, to the rear door and pushed in there. This is not the Diva entrance I had hoped for.

I now salute the wheelchair pushers of the world. I think they are saints! They put you in your chair, gather your belongings, get you comfortable, and then off you go, often fighting for your way in between hordes of passengers, many approaching with the speed of a wildebeest migration. They wait patiently outside the Ladies' Room for you and then continue the journey to the plane.

One other observation is that when you are sitting in the wheelchair, it is hard to feel totally elegant and dignified. The foot pedals are spread far apart, so it is impossible to sit without your feet spread apart. Your knees won't meet. I am reminded of my old twelfth-grade English teacher, Miss McNeil, who always wore a skirt and sat with her legs apart. We could all see her underwear, which at the time was a big source of hilarity. I feel a bit like Miss McNeil as I travel through the airport.

At times, my agent would park me somewhere and say, "I'll come and get you when it is time to board." In the morning of the Aegean flight, I was parked too far from the Ladies' Room to think I could make it on my own, and I really needed to go! I just had to hold it and hope for the best. I was also a few feet from a coffee and bakery place, and the smell of fresh coffee was driving me crazy with desire for a fresh brew. I hadn't had breakfast. I was like the big dog with its paws up on the kitchen counter and able to see the steak, but unable to reach it. I wanted to ask a nice-looking soul if they would buy me a coffee, but I lost my nerve each time I spotted a possible candidate. Everyone else looked so able-bodied. What a wake-up call for me to be empathetic to others in this condition.

By the way, I was never abandoned. The wheelchair agents always showed up with their iPads in time to transfer me on board, or through customs and immigration.

Another confession: As I hobbled along in my boot and one good leg, crutches or poles for support, slow and slightly stooped, I had a vision of what I might look like as old. I mean, *really* old. Perhaps ninety-four instead of eighty-four. Perhaps frail. Even without my red hair (OMG no!). I felt vulnerable. Is this what it's like? To be injured? Broken? Dependent on others? Are the glory days over?

At first, that scared the living daylights out of me, but then I accepted it. One day it may be so.

Each day, it seems I am crossing another threshold, going through another door as I face and deal with the process of getting older.

CHAPTER 26
Getting Back Up on the Horse

My experience in Santorini was a wake-up call. I am not unbreakable. My ankle can attest to that. Upon returning home, I visited my doctor for follow-up care and learned that I would need to wear a boot for at least six weeks, followed by approximately six weeks of physical therapy.

I taught my first class back at UNLV via Zoom, but the following week, I took an Uber to campus to teach in person. The class gave me a welcome-back card with lovely messages written on it. But in truth, it was difficult to get about and continue the pace I was used to. Even though I was grateful that my injury had not been worse.

I was also starting to have some eyesight problems, which made driving at night difficult. Oh no! Is this what it is like to get old? I had to ask to leave class a full hour early so I could make it home before sunset. Another blow to my ego.

But worse than that, I started to have fantasies of being injured on future trips, one of which was my upcoming holiday trip to Essaouira in Morocco, again with my sister Carol. At first, I told her I wanted to cancel, but she wisely advised me to hold off on making a decision. My imagination had gotten a bit out of hand as I envisioned all sorts of disasters! I pictured tumbles down stairs and broken hips, not to mention head-on collisions on the highways as we drove to our destination. I even had catastrophes in my dreams, which included enough scenarios of disaster to fill a whole season of horror films. I could never forgive myself if I let fear get the better of me. I realized I would always be afraid of travel if I didn't complete this next trip and prove to myself that I could do it. My ankle was better, and the boot was off. So the trip was on.

Upon arrival in Essaouira, we discovered that our room was located on the third floor of the hotel, one of the riads in the center of the old medina, built many years ago around a central court and, of course, without an elevator. However, I managed to climb up slowly. The lovely room turned out to overlook the rooftop terrace where breakfast was served, and from which we could see the ocean.

I was exceedingly cautious everywhere we walked, as there were cobblestones, steps, and uneven surfaces to navigate. I wore solid ankle-supporting sneakers the whole time, though usually sneakers are not my fashion choice. As each day went by, I became more relaxed. But I needed a symbolic triumph, and I found it on the beach at sunset. Just outside the Medina gates is a long, curving bay with a wide sandy beach where you can ride camels and beautiful Arabian horses. What a sight to see--beautiful sleek animals galloping along the water's edge, the wind lifting their tails and manes, the low sun making their beautiful coats glisten.

Carol got involved with photographing the sunset, but I headed right down to the water's edge, where the camels and their handlers were, and nego-tiated for my ride. You mount the camels while they are sitting on the sand, their thin legs neatly folded under them, but they get up on their hind legs first, so you are pitched forward at quite an angle. For a quick moment, I imagined another face plant in the sand! But then the camel gets his front legs up, and I was even. I suddenly felt exhilarated! I triumphantly rode my beast for twenty minutes, giving me plenty of time to take in the glistening blue water, the setting sun, and the white town of Essaouira just down the beach.

This symbolized my "getting back up on the horse" moment. It marked the moment when I felt "I've got this!". I came to believe that, though caution and smart choices are important, my accident was a one-off and that I could return to travel with energy and confidence.

Back in the saddle again!

CHAPTER 27
The Beginning of Letting Go

Two things happened in 2023 that rocked me back on my feet. My sister's husband was diagnosed with ALS (Lou Gehrig's Disease). A healthy man in his eighties, amazingly virile and energetic for his age, he went quickly from playing golf to being in a wheelchair to having diminished use of his extremities and then his voice. The idea that one's last days could suddenly be condemned to such a harsh and miserable decline scared me.

It seemed so random. It could happen to anyone. And once condemned, no way out but to endure it, which he did with great courage. But would I?

As I started to internalize Jim's illness, I got a bit paranoid. Any twitch of my leg, muscle spasm, or stiffness convinced me I had the early signs of ALS, MS, Parkinson's, or even Stiff Body Syndrome. I imagined any number of diseases which would be slow, possibly painful, and make my last years difficult beyond imagining.

And who would take care of me? As a widow with no children, that thought is never far from my mind. If you have a spouse, they get the job, whether they want it or not, and most do it with astounding grace. Being the caretaker is incredibly difficult, and sometimes the job lasts a long time. But a single oldster without family nearby?

The other person whose news affected me was that of my friend Pat, a friend in the neighborhood that I had known for fifteen years or more, and whom I often saw weekly at one of the dinner clubs. She told us that she felt she could no longer live alone in her house here and had chosen to go into an independent living facility in Arizona, near one of her daughters.

Of course, I personalized this too, as getting to this point in my life is one of the things that I dread. Though the letting go of beloved items and photos was painful for Pat, she was happy with her choice and that she had made it of her own volition. However, I was still disturbed by witnessing her coping with the transition.

I know that one day I will no longer be able to cook my own food, manage my own finances, or generally figure out which side is up. When I go to the mailbox in my pull-ups or nearly set the stove on fire… who will help me decide when that time is? Who will help me move when I am already in the wacky old broad territory? And more importantly, how will I ever be able to give up my house and move into a small apartment in a facility, where I will be apart from my neighborhood friends?

I started to look around at my 2850-square-foot house and imagine being only able to take what would fit into a small one-bedroom apartment (or even a studio, worst case scenario). I look at the artwork on the walls and wonder which pieces I would choose.

Then I noticed examples of oldsters *not* letting go such as my neighbor who passed away after along and active life. Her son came to clear out her house, and what an ordeal it turned out to be. The garage was stuffed to the rooftop with boxes and boxes of memorabilia, old magazines, awards, blankets, files, and more. He seemed so overwhelmed. "What can I do to help" I asked.

"Come inside" he said. "What do I do with all this?" There were more and more "things" to discard, rehome, or just dump. Along one wall was a floor to ceiling display cabinet holding every size and shape of knick-knacks—figurines, cups, dolls, vases. Every corner of the living room had a bookshelf, side table, or shelf unit, all displaying photos, bric-a-brac and more "objets d'art". The kitchen cabinets were full of multiple china sets, glassware sets, bowls—not an inch of space.

I was able to find a thrift shop attached to a pet adoption place that was glad to come and get a few of the things, as some were good quality and might make a sale or two to benefit the animals. Nice photo frames are also of value to resell. But other than that, each area had to be emptied and for the most part, discarded.

"So, get a grip, Diana," I thought to myself. I will not leave my house so full of stuff that someone has a huge mountain of things to sort through and dispose of. It will undoubtedly be my two nieces from Canada, and though I plan to leave them some chocolate cake and champagne in the refrigerator, I don't want the clean-out to be a month-long job.

But the dilemma is letting go of the past. I, too, am guilty of hanging on to evidence of my life's work (if guilt is the appropriate word). I have boxes and boxes full of memorabilia attached to my career of performing as a dancer and actress and designing costumes for over sixty years.

Many shelves contain three-ring binders full of photos of plays I designed for with accompanying theater programs, press, and critics' reviews.

I embarked on a program, with fabulous assistance from my good friend Amber to digitize it all so I can at least throw away the hard copies. Keep or toss? Even throwing out the 8 x 10 glossies seems sacrosanct. Beautiful production shots from small productions forty to fifty years ago. How can I? Photos of actors I costumed, such as Ralph Meeker, Charles Durning, Richard Thomas, Harold Gould, Jill Clayberg, Salome Jens, Paula Prentiss, Sandy Dennis, Elizabeth Ashley, Susan Anspach, and so many more

I find keeping the items is a sort of "proof of life" while I am alive. Once I am gone, they can go in the dumpster, as I don't believe anyone will want them, nor will the items offer any information of such cultural significance that they should be kept. And I won't be around to witness the dumping. Though perhaps my hand will reach back from the beyond to pluck back a few favorite items, the way it happens when I make a donation to Goodwill.

One thing I have learned from this process, though, is that I was a much better designer than I ever gave myself credit for. Looking at photos of these plays that I did very early in my costume career, I am impressed. "Damn, Diana, you were actually really good!" I think, as I pat myself on the back. The actors look perfectly costumed for their roles. I honestly didn't know I was that good early in my design career.

Other items provide agonizing decisions to be made. What about my wedding gown? It was, when it arrived on my doorstep some forty-five years ago in plain brown wrapping, an authentic, 1905 silk afternoon tea gown of my grandmother's, the one who died before I was born. It is of the softest cream color with tiny pink roses all over it. It still had the original maker's name inside and the original whale boning, not plastic.

I was determined, as an "old" bride at fifty, not to wear a white frou-frou dress with a huge skirt and puffed sleeves. I wasn't even sure I wanted to wear white, and of course, I wanted to wear something dramatically different.

As my wedding gift, Bob Mackie, for whom I worked at the time, had one of his top costume makers fit the gown to me, and surprisingly, it fit well. We added one ruffle to the hem as I was tall. We removed the 1903 pigeon front to make it look more contemporary. Very little else was done or added, so the materials are all 125 years old. Only the reconstruction of the bodice makes it no longer authentic to the period.

Who should I give it to? This gown is special, not only because it was my wedding gown, but because it is an exquisite garment in its own right. I am still working on finding a suitable new home for it.

My cherry-red embroidered kimono, which I bought in Beijing, the one I adored but hesitated to buy because of its price, until famed costume designer Albert Wolsky told me, "You'll regret it if you don't purchase it!" He was right. I wore it once to the Costume Designers Guild Awards and now it still hangs in my closet.

The other part of letting go has to do with old habits, many ingrained from my upbringing. The struggle to achieve becomes an addiction. I am a serial achiever.

I have an inability to be still and to let go of the old habits of my work ethic. Why can't I go to the movies in the middle of the week, or always feel better on a day when I have "accomplished something"? I ask myself, "What did you *do* today?" not "What did you experience today," or "What did you enjoy today?" I bear the burden of high expectations of myself.

My cat Nala has no problem with enjoying each day as it comes.

"Why can't you be more like me?" Nala says. "I get up when you get up, eat a little breakfast, and give myself a bath. Then I find a favorite spot for my first nap of the day.

Later, I look out the window at the birds flitting about in the backyard (and wish I could get my paws on them), and sometimes I watch over you when you swim. I exercise by doing some zoomies up the stairs and back down at full speed. In the afternoon, I like to lie in the guest room where the afternoon sun comes in the French door window and warms the carpet.

Around 5 pm, I come upstairs and tell you it's time to quit sewing or writing and come downstairs. After dinner, I curl up on the sofa next to you and watch TV.

See? It's not so hard." I accomplish absolutely nothing and yet am loved and adored."

Nala taking one of her many daily naps

CHAPTER 28
What's a Girl To Wear In Her Eighties?

I was sitting one day at Einstein Bros. Bagels enjoying an iced coffee, and an elderly woman, at least in her eighties, approached. She looked so smart in a simple tan dress with a pattern of black leaves on it that I had to comment,

"How nice you look!"

"Really? Thank you, thank you! And I love your pants. They remind me of sunshine and good things".

That made my day. I love to think I have made someone think of "sunshine and good things" with my pink, yellow, and blue Pucci-like print jersey pants I made earlier that week.

To me, clothing is an expression of one's soul, one's personality, and one's artistic spirit. One's sense of humor. It is a powerful means of communication. Why should that change as we get older?

I see older women's surrender of colorful and stylish clothing in favor of effortless shorts and t-shirts devoted entirely to comfort. We wear so much grey in the US. But to me, color is uplifting and life-affirming.

One time, back in Los Angeles, I was invited to dinner with a friend who had also invited Tony Curtis (yes, that Tony Curtis). I arrived at the restaurant in a breezy yellow dress with small pink flowers on it. "Dahling, you look like spring!" Tony exclaimed in his New York accent. Afterwards, Dominic used to imitate him frequently whenever I wore something fresh and colorful.

Fashion magazines mostly show young and slim models showing off the fashion lines amid the ads for anti-aging creams and other miracle-working ointments. It's hard to feel noticed or worthy of wearing and buying the styles, even though older women often have much more disposable income to purchase these items. Our culture doesn't encourage older women to have fun with their clothing, which I think is sad indeed. But note, style and fashion are not the same. We don't need to be slaves to seasonal trends to be stylish. It is a very real cultural phenomenon that elders feel invisible, but sometimes I think they dress to be invisible, to succumb to that scenario. I don't mean you have to dress ablaze in neon color, but if you look like your clothing decisions were made by the Committee of Grey, why not consider a refresh?

And now that I am in my eighties, what adjustments have I made in deference to my advancing years?

Well, shoes, for sure. I've always had broad feet and a bit of a bunion from my years as a dancer, so I never wanted to draw attention to my feet. I was never the one who had the bright red sandals or the yellow pumps. I stuck to black, white, and "nude" colors pretty much all my life, and it remains the same. But now it's flats or wedges, gentle ones. But if 4-inch heels were made to be comfortable for eighty-year-old legs and feet, you can bet I'd be wearing them.

Nowadays, women my age just want to be comfortable. I understand. We've earned it. I grew up in the fifties and had to wear those white cotton bras with circular stitching and a band that had absolutely no elasticity to it. Occasionally, I wore a waist cincher and even a girdle, which gave one a nice flat bum. At age fourteen, my mother told me, "It's unladylike for a woman to show the curves of her buttocks."

And the ultimate sartorial torture was the dreaded garter belt. Made of non-stretchy cotton or satin, it lay just below the waist. Stockings were attached by four dangling pieces of elastic and metal garter clips. I had no curvy hips to keep the belt up, so I had to fasten it really tight. When I took the miserable thing off after a long day, I had red welts around my upper hips.

Spandex wasn't invented until the late fifties and was not used in bras and other underwear until the mid-sixties. Pantyhose were still in the future and were invented once skirts rose to such heights as to require them for some semblance of modesty.

However, while growing up and still at home, my mother strictly regulated my shopping for clothing. Once in spring and once in the fall, she helped me make a list before shopping for new clothes. The list was divided into three columns. In one column, we listed the "Haves" -what I already had in the way of a good travel suit, a day dress, an afternoon dress, slacks for weekends, etc. The second column was headed "Needs," with entries such as "could use a new day dress or two for winter, needs a new winter coat, could use a couple of sweaters." The third column was, of course, my favorite! It was headed "Wants," and in this column, I had plenty of entries… a poodle skirt, a black sheath dress-up dress, more pants, etc. Only after we had fulfilled the "Needs" column could I choose one or two from the "Wants" column. And all this before we even headed out.

This was still the day when one's clothing was very much formalized into what was suitable for the occasion. Pants were only acceptable for working in the garden or on the weekends in the country. There was such a thing as an afternoon dress, which I assume was perfect for a tea party. Then there was a cocktail dress and an evening dress, and God forbid you wore the wrong thing at the wrong time. White gloves were still worn to go downtown shopping, can you believe it? In fact, in my four years at university, I only wore pants to class one time, and that was because there had been a blizzard, and I wanted to wear my ski pants. Don't think I didn't get lots of stares.

When I left home in 1961 to join *My Fair Lady*, my outfits were still very proper, but as the decade progressed and we entered the swinging sixties, skirts got shorter, and colors got brighter. By now, I was on my own, working on Broadway or on tour with a play, and did not have to answer to anyone. I could wear just about anything I wanted. I was also at the peak of my youthful fitness and appeal. In other words, I had a hot body back then!

In 1965, I remember seeing my very first pantsuit.

It was in December of 1965 when an actress named Diane Aubrey arrived from London to start rehearsals for the National Company of "The Odd Couple." At the time, I was the understudy for both characters, Gwendolyn and Cecily Pigeon. Diane was blond and beautiful and reminded me of Julie Christie. She wore dress pants and a matching tailored jacket made from a beautiful, subtle grey and heather blue plaid. I was transfixed! I had never seen an outfit like it, as at this time, there were no pantsuits on the market in the US or even on the fashion pages. At least none had come before my eyes.

I could not *wait* to find something similar. The idea of a suit with pants that was an entire matching ensemble seemed brilliant to me—why had no one thought of this before for women? It was a few months before I found one, and I immediately bought it. I wore it constantly, very often, with a turtleneck sweater, soft ankle boots in a matching tan color, and my tan leather gloves.

Diana posing in her newly purchased pantsuit
Photo by Dick Epperson

Once relocated to California in the 1970s, I found it a wild, colorful, changing society. I wore lots of jeans, which you could buy for $7.00 a pair at the hippest stores (the original Fred Segal on Melrose and Crescent Heights). However, one day, I was invited to Jane Fonda's house. Yes, I am name-dropping, but the fact that it was Jane Fonda is relevant. It was a meeting to discuss Women's Rights at a time when the subject matter was very much in the forefront. Gloria Steinem, Erica Jong, and others were writing books we all devoured.

Anyway, there were about thirty women at the meeting, all loudly claiming that women needed the freedom to make their own choices. And yet I noticed that every single one of them was wearing blue jeans and a white T-shirt (I was in a dress.). It occurred to me that they were slaves to the "uniform" of the young, hip, socially enlightened ERA-promoting, pro-choice women, and somehow, I saw no choice or freedom of expression in what they chose to wear. They were like sheep.

It was probably silly of me, but I vowed that night that I would never wear jeans again, and I never have. I told you it was silly, but it's my own little declaration of independence.

Instead, I wore mini dresses with matching fabric panties or long bell-bottom pants over high wedge sandals, which made me about 6 feet tall. My hair was down to my waist.

I even opened a small boutique on La Cienega Boulevard near Melrose Avenue called (what a surprise) "Eden" with a logo that looks very similar to the Apple.com logo (I did it first). I specialized in patchwork dresses, which were the rage at the time, and I got an LA Times Weekend Magazine cover story out of it.

In the 1980s, when I was just starting up the ladder of costume design success, I loved the power suits and pantsuits. They were so easy to wear because the outfit was pre-ordained to look complete with just the addition of a blouse. I felt streamlined and well-put-together without too much trouble. I miss my professional pantsuits.

In the mid-80s, I was costume designing full-time for prime-time TV series. Unlike what this job title may lead you to believe, I did not spend hours sketching and sewing period costumes for historical dramas. My field was contemporary design, which meant contemporary fashion, but specifically geared towards illustrating the character of the actor I was dressing.

I spent many hours each day in the stores looking for the fashion pieces that, once assembled uniquely for an actor-- perhaps altered, dyed, trimmed, and fitted to the performer--were now officially a "costume." From my first show in 1985, *The Facts of Life*, where I shopped for the characters, Mrs. Garrett, Tootie, Blair, Jo, and Natalie, until my last show, *Passions*, ended in 2008, I shopped and shopped.

Many people are dismissive of shopping as part of the costume designer's job. Still, it is an essential part of the job unless you are designing a period piece like *Bridgerton*. In the same way, a set designer uses purchased furniture, artwork, dinner dishes accessories on the tables, and just about everything to create a brand-new set, so do costume designers buy existing pieces. We find the styles that work for each character and help tell the story. Once we have individualized them after an in-depth fitting process and collaboration with the actor, then we can claim to have created their "costume."

I prefer this process to historical design, where one must conform to historical standards of shape, detail, silhouette, fabric, and decoration. In contemporary design, I must really understand my character's psyche and make choices that reveal to audiences what is going on in that character's mind. I feel that sometimes I am a clothing psychologist. So, you can see I have spent many years of my adult life around clothes of all kinds. And now? Are sweatsuits the pantsuits of retirement? My God, I hope not.

When I moved to Las Vegas, I realized quickly that retirement clothes were another ball of wax. Wearing a black pantsuit and a little grey silk blouse to Home Depot just seemed weird. And it was. I ran into a neighbor one day and was wearing a leopard print jersey-knit dress from Ross for Less, nothing fancy. She said, "Wow, you're dressed up. Where are you off to?"

So now, working my way through my 80s, what's a girl to wear?

Surely, it can't all be about comfort. Is there no fun with textiles, prints, colors, and shapes anymore? The reason we even wear clothing, after modesty and protection from the elements, is personal expression. And I want to express myself!

I saw this meme on Facebook. It said, "The only thing you shouldn't wear after sixty is the weight of other people's opinions." So true. Enjoying style as we get older is often reframed to shame those of us who love clothing into thinking we are not accepting ourselves as we are, sagging, bulgy, and wrinkly. With that assumption is a touch of judgment. It is as if those of us who are interested in our outward garments are not conforming to societal expectations. As if we are married to looking young and are not suitably examining our inner lives.

Can't I do both? Clothes are fun! Clothes are language. It's about authenticity and embracing one's individuality. If you are living your older life with energy and curiosity, why can't your clothes reflect that? I'd rather be a bit eccentric than boring. I want to age with style.

Me wearing one of my fun print dresses,
royal blue and bright yellow for Santorini

CHAPTER 29
The Silver Tea Set

I went to make a note in my to-do list, and my pen lit up. It illuminated a little sign that said, "My will was signed at Smith & Johnson Law Firm." Well, that's one way to be reminded that life is short.

But it's true. I recently re-did my will—nothing radical—just keeping it up to date. I have always been organized. When I am getting ready to go on a long trip, I research everything, make endless lists, and ensure everything is in order before heading for the airport. And what is aging and dying but one long trip?

Recently, ads have come across my social feed for the Nokbox, which I figured out means the Next of Kin box. I thought about organizing my accounts, lists, and passwords to pass on in an orderly manner to whoever my survivors are. I won't go as far as writing my own obit (though I do have some awfully good bios in a folder called "bios and resumes" on my computer) or ordering the crustless cucumber sandwiches to be served after my funeral... but close. (And please serve ice cream too.)

Then I remembered I started a similar book for Dominic. Recently, when I got that book out, I discovered I bought the book barely one month before Dominic died.

You see, it never occurred to either of us that he would die before me. As I was thirteen and half years older than he, it seemed obvious that I would go first. That was the plan. We used to joke that I arranged it this way so that I didn't have to be the widow when he went. It seemed only fair. He was a flirt, handsome, and much more likely to find a new partner than I would be. I used to say that the ideal plan would be for us to die together on our way home from a wonderful vacation, sunburned and exhausted, with details to follow.

But death isn't fair, as we all know. Our great plan didn't work out.

So, at eighty-four, I updated and signed my new will, which is actually a living trust. I wasn't quite clear on the difference, but my lawyer assured me a trust was better, especially since my assets are here in the US and all my beneficiaries are across the border in Toronto. I simplified everything, making sure I divided up the spoils in the way I wanted, assigned a power of attorney for when I get dotty, and wrote a solid DNR (*Do Not Resuscitate*). I am adamant about the DNR.

Apparently, somewhere around seventy percent of US citizens don't have a will. I am always surprised to find that many of my friends don't have wills. "Well," they say, "I know I *should* have one, but I won't have that much to leave anyway, and the court will figure it all out." Others say, "I get upset having to think about it." Or, "My only child gets everything, so why do I need a will?"

I've had a will since about the age of forty, at least since both my parents died and left me a small amount of money. But I have always enjoyed updating my will, as it makes me feel very munificent, as though I am going to make many people happy with my "lavish" gifts, a regular Bill Gates in a skirt.

I picture a crusty old lawyer in a three-piece suit gathering the family members around in an old wood-paneled library and announcing, "Your great-aunt Diana has bequeathed you the painting of the sailboats, and to you, the silver tea set," etc., etc. I have less than a dozen items of any value, so I haven't minded deciding who gets what. It's almost been like a game.

Of course, lifestyles have changed, and I doubt any nieces or nephews *want* the silver tea sets or paintings. And I don't have diamonds and emeralds to disperse. Sorry.

My parents were always very organized about their wills. When they downsized from the family home, my father organized a system of colored round stickers, one color for each of us three siblings, so we could attach them to the underside of furniture to identify what would eventually go to us.

My mother, who knew she was terminal with her lung cancer, laid out all her jewelry on the bed one day and had my sister and me come in and choose our favorite pieces, me first as I was the oldest, then Carol, then me, and so forth.

She did the same with the silver, crystal, and the fine china. I was very eager to get every single piece that was my share, but mainly because of my inferiority complex when it came to taking my rightful place in the Toronto hierarchy. Since I left at age twenty-one to basically "join the circus," I always felt the family looked down on me socially.

My mother pouring tea, (England 1940s) as she did
every afternoon for the rest of her life

I left an elegant life with oriental rugs on the floor, mahogany furniture topped with crystal vases holding flowers from the garden. Once adults, we had a glass of sherry before going into the dining room for dinner where we used the good silver and cloth napkins. I left manners, convention, and expectations of life continuing in the same way forever. My next home, if I had stayed in Toronto, would have been a nice small apartment somewhere, furnished with leftovers from my parents' home, things they no longer needed, but still in the same vein.

Instead, I lived in New York in a fourth-floor walk-up apartment, collected unemployment insurance between jobs (my father called it "the dole"), and worked as a cocktail waitress when needed. The apartment had no oriental rugs nor mahogany furniture - indeed, it was just bits of things I could find on the street on trash day. I'm not sure where my bed came from, but the springs and mattress were so old and bowed in the middle it was like sleeping in a hammock. The curtains for the back window, which looked out over the fire escape, were shower curtains as they were cheaper than real curtains. During the same period, my university classmates were marrying well, being set up in nice houses by their in-laws, and decorating them in a way that repeated what they had grown up with

But I wanted a career on the stage in New York. My mother once referred to my life as "nomadic," a description which stung and which I never forgot or forgave. As if I were living in a Bedouin tent and herding goats. Or riding the rails! If there was a big giveaway going on of family stuff, she would say, "But it makes no sense to ship it all those miles and *across the border*."

I was greedy for all the spoils that I felt were rightfully mine, mostly to buoy up my feelings that I was equally worthy as my two siblings. But it seems I wasn't in my mother's eyes.

I was left out of one really valuable item. My mother's family has owned a forty-three-acre island since 1883, or thereabouts, located three hours north of Toronto in the lake district of Muskoka, a very popular summer cottage region. It was a virgin forest, with only two structures on it, the "Big House," as it was called, a rambling two-story house with many bedrooms, servants' quarters, and a verandah running around the circumference, and my mother's cottage, built initially as my grandfathers' gym. My uncle left his half of the island to my brother, Bill, and my mother left her half to my sister. I was left out entirely. As my mother explained, "You have left Canada, probably won't return, and would only want a part of the island to sell."

I feel this was punishment for rejecting the Toronto lifestyle. Some may see this differently, but this is my emotional truth, and so I share it. It hurt.

"Lighten up, Diana," I say to myself now. "You probably couldn't have afforded the property taxes anyway."

Now, the gold-leaf china and my wedding china sit in my kitchen cupboard, worthless on eBay. The damask tablecloths went to a friend who loves to entertain, and the stemware will go to a friend who is starting up a film props collection. Perhaps a film depicting the Gilded Age will need these fine place settings.

There is a certain feeling of obligation when you have children to leave the family heirlooms to them, and so my first will carefully divided up these items I fought for amongst my nieces and nephews. I was careful to be fair and assign a relatively equal value to each one.

As time went on, I realized that without children who will be *expecting* certain items from the family, I am really free to leave whatever I want to whomever would be most grateful to have the items. So, I put far less in the will as these items are all outdated anyway. What would a man or woman in today's world *want* with a silver tea set?

Honestly, we all just have too much stuff. We think this is our physical legacy, the things we inherited from our parents and grandparents and have protected all these years, but which now have little value to anyone. We have our medals, awards, and certificates of achievement. We have our photos. Really, no one wants these? Of course not, they have only buoyed up our own sense of self-importance.

Many Americans have a nice enough standard of living to have homes big enough to fill with boxes and boxes of memories, important only to them. In most places in the country, houses have basements, which I am convinced were designed to encourage a ton of hoarding. In Las Vegas, we have no basements, so the garage becomes the hoarding place of choice. Some people even have storage lockers off-site in which things they can't let go of get housed, with a monthly payment to boot.

We spend our lives gathering things, only to have to dispose of them. But without children, who will get these things? One assumes only the children will care, and most of the time, they really don't. So, who will I leave my most precious memories to?

I find asking friends or young folk what they would like to have of mine makes them very uncomfortable. Especially the younger ones. "Oh, you are going to live forever," they will quickly say, or "I don't want to think about that." Or, they will think you are harboring news of some imminent and terminal disease. I must find a way to handle this better. I have left a note that my closest friends can come over and take anything they want, and then the rest of my neighbors in the community can come and take anything. Whether a chest of drawers or a salad spinner *Any*thing!

Also included in my Last Will and Testament is my DNR. Do *not* resuscitate! Please, should I become ill or have some kind of medical emergency, do *not* patch me up and return me to the arms of my waiting nursing-home worker, to survive a bit longer stuck in a wheelchair watching those daytime TV shows I hate. It would be different if I had a husband who needed me or children, but at the age of eighty-five onward, I am not interested in operations, procedures, radiations, medicines, infusions, and treatments that would prolong a life once adventurous into one of prolonged discomfort. If I am indeed alive, I still want a life of worth and purpose.

Atul Gawande says, in his remarkable book *Being Mortal*, that the focus of today's medicine is to concentrate on fixing things, on repairing our health. Often the last months of our lives are spent in treatments that exhaust our bodies and emotions with very little benefit or quality of life.

My dad was a devoted doctor all of his life. I wish I could talk to him about this. I wonder what he would think.

In this esteemed document, my will, I have also indicated my wishes for what to do with me. After I am gone, that is.

I am not much of a fan of funerals, though I do understand their necessity in helping the family deal with the loss. I have requested cremation and a scattering of the ashes somewhere warm. (Isn't it ridiculous to think that I am worrying about my ashes feeling cold, or claustrophobic from being buried underground? Or that I'd feel terrible if I kept lying there in a cemetery, and no one ever came to visit me!) Perhaps I prefer to think of my ashes as my own kind of fairy dust, that will go into the world and entertain people or inspire them.

No funeral for me either. But a big party? Yes indeed! As long as I am not the last one standing, by all means, come and celebrate me. Have a party. Eat good food. *Wear bright colors.* And tell everyone that I had an impact.

CHAPTER 30
The Last One Standing

I don't fear the storm.

In fact, let it roar through my home, tear at my roof, shatter my windows. Let lightning flash with blinding brilliance and burn me, let thunder roar and crack with shocking power. Let it scare me. I welcome it. I welcome the wind that bows the trees and threatens to topple them across my path, across my house, across my very being. Bring it on.

What I fear is the silence. The quiet of days spent alone, waiting for the next day, which will also be spent alone. The endless monotony of eventlessness.

I don't fear violence. The violence of criminals exploding with rage against their world, against their government, and against their fruitless life. Bring it on. Let them break into my house, smash my windows, and invade my space. I'm not afraid. I will welcome them and their anger as an antidote to the monotony of my day-to-day solitude. Their rage will match my rage at a declining life, once full of excitement and extraordinary events that fueled my energy to live.

I fear the plainness. The average-ness. The repetitive day-to-day existence, as my friends start to die. One by one, they go before me. My greatest fear. Why am I so healthy? I want to die while my friends can still gather and wail about my loss, and scream with laughter about my funny habits. But one by one, they go before me. My circle gets smaller and smaller, like the watering hole that dries up and shrinks to nothing as the drought consumes all.

I don't fear the noise, the uproar. I want it. Let me feel the heat of chaos. I fear more the coldness of long days, wrapped in a shawl to keep out the drafts. Of the shrinking world. Where my only humans are patronizing nurses who say 'How are we today?' People in the next room watch television with dead-eyed stupor, watch shows that blare false energy and excitement over guessing the price of a refrigerator.

I fear the quiet. I fear the loss. I fear being the last one standing. I fear others making the decisions for me. "We know what is best for you". I fear losing physical agility. I fear losing mental acuity. I fear losing joy, I fear losing the energy that comes from feeling useful and creative.

Let me have just enough freedom to walk out into the desert alone. Let me lie down under a gnarly tree and let the sun bake down on me until I can't stand the heat any longer. Let me relinquish my last breath. Then let the wild animals come and tear me apart. Let them feast from my body, break my bones, and lick my blood. At least I will live again in the arteries of a mountain lion, alive to crawl along a mountain ridge at dawn.

CHAPTER 31
When Is It Time?

The first time I read this poem "The Last One Standing" was at the Summer Writing Conference of the International Women's Writers Guild in 2024. I was worried that it might be too self-indulgent, too intense. But as I looked out into the audience, I could see women nodding their heads. It was then that I knew that I was not alone, and that many of us have to face this fear head-on. In fact, this fear is what inspired me to write this book.

Okay, the poem presents the *worst* of my fears. Chalk it up to a cloudy day when I wrote it. Bette Davis is attributed with first saying, "Old age ain't no place for sissies."

Living in a fifty-five-and-older community as I do, I am surrounded by the most wonderful neighbors, all of similar ages to me and mostly retired. We socialize with each other and, more importantly, we look out for each other. It has been a blessing. I don't know what I would have done after Dominic died without their support.

The other side of the coin is that most of us are in the "Final Fifth" of our lives with all the attendant crises. The moment an ambulance shows up in the 'hood, we are all wondering, who is it? "Is it so-and-so who has fallen again?" "I hear Mrs. Smith has been having mini-strokes." "Oh-oh, Sam must have gone off his meds again." Usually, the nosiest of neighbors is sent to check out who is headed for the hospital, and we secretly find relief that it's not us.

We are bombarded with the notion that illness, accidents, and emergencies of the worst type are inevitable, along with the loss of our independence. Am I to believe that I am headed toward the unavoidable decline, disintegration, and deterioration of my body and brain? Will my body parts start to squeak, leak, break, ache, shrink, expand, and generally make themselves known?

187

What if it is *not* true? In spite of what I see around me, what if, allowing for a few aches and pains, my brain stays active and engaged until the day I die? What if aging is full of possibilities, not just diminishment? As Eliza Doolittle sang, "Wouldn't that be loverly?"

As a single older woman without kids, my fear has been that my family is too far away from me to look after me, and indeed, I would not wish that burden on them. My sister is only a few years behind me in age, and my nieces and nephews are busy with their own young lives and careers, not to mention living three thousand miles away. So, who will tell me when I'm going wonky and it's no longer safe to live in my own house? And will I believe them? I may have to be both the Elder-Needing-Care, *and* the Caregiver.

Will I become that cranky, stubborn "I can-still-do-this" person I will have to deal with, or will I leave my home without a fuss? Here's how it might go:

Caregiver Diana: I think it's time we talked about how you are doing.

Elder Diana: Why? Of course, I am doing just fine. Never better.

Caregiver Diana: Well, you left the stove on for the fourth time last week, and I think you might have eaten Nala's food instead of the meatloaf I left for you.

Elder Diana: Nonsense. And that meatloaf was delicious.

Caregiver Diana: I found you splayed out on the floor when I stopped by yesterday. I think it's those computer cords you keep strung in a big spaghetti mess near where you sit with your computer.

Elder Diana: No, no, that was my plank position. I was doing yoga. Stop worrying. It's bad enough you took my car keys away. I should never have let you do that. My Uber costs are going through the roof.

Caregiver Diana: I think it's time to talk about moving you into an Assisted Living Facility. You wouldn't have to think about your meals anymore, and you would have company and lots to do.

Elder: No, no, no! I love my house! I mean, I really, really love it! It's just the way I want it, and even though I can't get upstairs anymore, I still use each room downstairs, and adore looking out at my pool. I love my artwork on the walls, and all the little treasures I have brought back from my travels. Each one makes me smile.

Caregiver Diana: But you will be able to take some of those.

Elder Diana: Huh! Are you kidding? How can the contents of a 2800-

square-foot house fit in a small one-bedroom apartment? Impossible! How will I choose?

Caregiver Diana: We will help you. And think of all the activities you will have -- crafting, movies, book readings. I hear they even bring in a clown for birthday parties.

Elder: Oh my God! Don't send in the clown! And that's not the worst of it. I'm afraid they will get me up at seven every morning, a time when no sane person gets up, and then make me take medicines, and do sing-alongs, or park me in front of a TV when they know I can't abide daytime game shows.

CG: Well, at least you will have company for dinner every night.

Elder: Yes, but will they let me have my vodka and tonic before dinner? And what if the conversation is inane? What if I am seated with The Mean Girls or The Grudge Keepers, who do nothing but complain about how everything used to be better in the old days?

What if the movies they show are things like "It's a Wonderful Life" rather than the contemporary dramas and action shows I like? What if there are no lectures to keep my brain agile? I can't do this. I will miss my friends too much. And then I wonder if I will see young people again? And worst of all, I'm not sure they will let me take Nala. I could never leave her behind.

Elder Diana's resistance is understandable. Leaving her home, her refuge, is a painful transition for her. At home, she is in charge. It's the one place where her own priorities are honored. But moving her out would mean less danger of injury and less stress for everyone involved. And selling her house would provide her with an income to offset the cost of Assisted Living.

It is far from the time I will have to consider this, as I am blessed with good health right now and am quite capable of taking care of myself, but just to allay my fears, I thought I would go and visit one of the local assisted living facilities.

I approach the building with an open heart and an open mind. As I walk in, I enter a nice foyer with a high ceiling, walls brightly painted white, and everything looking fresh and clean.

The first three people I saw were in wheelchairs or were supported with walkers. "Don't judge Diana," I said to myself, "you'll be there one day. Remember Greece?" My guide arrived and was very charming, and we started the tour. We passed the dining room where I saw a woman eating at a table by herself. But there were other groups of two, three, and four eating together. Then we moved on to an area they were renovating, which she said would be like a sports bar with a television for games and bar food. "This is more my style," I thought. "As long as they show football. Even at ninety-two, I'll be able to enjoy the sight of those magnificently fit men in their tight pants, leaping up with a long arm to catch the football, sailing down the field from many yards away".

Down the hallway we walked and into the library, which had comfortable seats and looked like a good place to hang out. So far, so good. Then I saw one of the apartments. What could one expect? It was small, just enough for a sofa, a TV, and a little mini table, perhaps for my computer. The kitchenette had just enough space for one to make breakfast. The bedroom was small but adequate, and the bathroom likewise, but no bathtub! I love my baths! Of course, no bathtub for safety's sake… for the elderly.

Now that I've seen the spaces are bright and clean, I said to the residence representative, "I am more concerned about the philosophy of this place. I don't want a residence that will infantilize me. Do you have visiting lecturers?"

"No," she said.

"What about language classes?"

"No," she said, "but you could form an informal group if you find other people wanting to practice a language." Good.

"What do you do to keep the residents' brains active?"

"Oh, we have brain games once a week. We play 'Name That Tune.'" Oh my God, once again, looking back at the past. I wasn't really thinking quite along those lines.

And now we enter the movie theater room, which is a good size and has about twenty very comfortable-looking brown chairs and a large screen. I look at the walls and I can't help myself. I guffawed out loud! There is a poster of… *It's A Wonderful Life!* And all the other movie posters were from films from the 1940s and 50s.

At that moment, I knew that *this particular* assisted living home would not be for me. Maybe another one somewhere else. I don't want to live in nostalgia-land. But the idea of people to socialize with does appeal to me.

In Judith Viorst's book *Making the Best of What's Left: When We're*

Too Old to Get the Chairs Reupholstered, she says her residence has committees to serve on, musical performances (Basie to Bach); guest lectures (about politics, science, art). There are also discussion groups (current events, fiction, nonfiction). This sounds better.

A week later I got an email from a gentleman who runs a program he has called the Carnegie College at his Independent Living residence. He booked me to give a lecture about my career in Costume Design! So there is reason for hope. This time I'll be the lectur*er*, but one day I will be the lectur*ee*.

What I do know is that social connections are one of the most important things for happiness in later life. Places like these would afford me opportunities to have friends and activities. I know myself. Pretty soon, I would be organizing trips to the ballet, writing the residents' newsletter.

But what are the alternatives?

For many years, I have had this fantasy that I would buy a huge villa in the South of France and invite a select number of dance and film students to come and stay for free in the many rooms this villa would have. I would be up in a wing somewhere, totally autonomous, with a person to help with my medical needs. There would be a pool, of course, which the "kids" could use, and lectures, dance classes, and film screenings. Food would be plentiful and available twenty-four hours a day. From my top-floor perch, I would hear the voices of the students, perhaps some of their music, and from time to time, I would come down to visit with them. I would ask them what kind of classes they wanted, what films I should rent for them, and if they needed me for any life advice, which I would willingly give.

Ah, how wonderful that would be. But it would require a boatload of money.

Another alternative, perhaps still fantasy, is to live in a "commune" with people I *already* know rather than having to make new friends all over again. I hate being forever "the new girl". Why live among strangers? What about chosen family? If we all age out at the same time, maybe we can do this?

Two people, very dear to me, have recently told me about their specially formed circle of friends who looked after a woman, their friend, until near the end. They organized and took turns with the various jobs that needed doing——laundry, groceries, doctors' visits, and companionship.

What a gift, and what an amazing group of women to do this. What an example of people who didn't pawn the job off to a medical institution but took it on themselves. I am in awe.

And I must be around young people, at least some of the time. I can see myself showing up at UNLV, being ferried there in a senior bus of some kind, hobbling up the steps of the FDH Building, then sitting in the back of the theater during my old Film Advanced Directing Class, so I can see what the kids are up to. Just to be around them. They won't know who the old fart in the back row is!

The biggest takeaway for me has been that to conquer fear, one must drag the feared scenario out of the cave and face it head-on. My fear of losing independence and joy in the last few years of my life is what propelled me to write this book. However, as I have examined some of the variables and possibilities, I have come to feel less anxious about it. I know that I have *some* control over choices for the future, but not all, and that if I am to be a woman of character, I will accept what comes. Looking at things in the light has made things less terrifying and more manageable. Heck, I may even turn out to be a sweet old lady after all!

One of my favorite prayers is the Serenity Prayer. "Grant me the serenity to know the things I cannot change; the courage to change the things I can; and the wisdom to know the difference." What a wonderful guideline to life these few words offer!

I cannot change getting old. I will make a plan for the things I can change, and I just hope I know the difference. At some point, I will have to say, "Get over yourself, Diana, and just deal with it".

CHAPTER 32
Praise the Women

Praise the women who have suffered, who've braved the loss of hair, the fear of chemo, the transition from their good life to dependence on doctors and nurses and caregivers and tubes and treatment and trials.

Praise the women who have lost a child, the worst of all scenarios, who've had to pass by the street corner daily where their beloved fell, never to recover.

Praise all the women in wheelchairs, scooters, and walkers that I saw when I visited an Assisted Living facility, and for whom, at the time, I felt no real connection.

Fuck me for not being more empathetic, for not facing that I too will be there sooner or later.

Bless the women who have lost siblings and close friends for they have felt their circle of family falling away, and damn me for avoiding the thought that I too will lose my brother and sister. I have lost several of my closest friends, but I am used to the feeling of being alone in the world.

Fuck me for sounding self-pitying.

Praise the women who have let their hair go grey, have become fat, and who wear no makeup.

Fuck me, I am not there yet. May never be.

Bless the women who have become caregivers, not through choice but through the unkind circumstances of life. Those who give up their own life and wonder when they will get it back. A medal of valour to them for giving up a normal life to fulfill their promises.

Fuck me for thinking I couldn't do it, and feeling fortunate that I haven't had to.

Kudos to the women who have wished for an exciting life and yet never had it, working hard all their lives without the rewards they sought, and looking towards a future without expectations. For a life invisible.

Bless the immigrant women, walking for days and weeks to reach a better life, and then not finding it. Bless the women of color who still feel the burdens of prejudice. Bless the women who keep going in spite of bombs and missiles falling on them in those countries torn by war or famine.

Fuck me for not being grateful every day of my life.

CHAPTER 33
REGRETS, I'VE HAD A FEW

While writing this book, I came across a paragraph from author Griffin Hansbury in his Oldster Magazine interview that affected me deeply. He says,

"Capitalism—and its wellness industry—insists that we always 'improve,' become healthier, happier, and more successful, keep striving for the myth of perfection, including some idea of a perfectly Zen and joyful mental state. But maybe the goal in life is to transform, as Freud famously put it, 'neurotic misery into ordinary unhappiness.' The only way I know to get there is through grieving, and getting older can be a process of moving through grief for all that gets lost along the way, including ideas about who we should be and how we should feel."

All that gets lost along the way? It seems that self-improvement and or wisdom is an ongoing job with no end in sight. I thought I'd arrived in the hammock at the end of my last book, but apparently not. I am taking stock of my life, but at this stage, my story is written. There is no re-living or re-framing it, much as I might want to. Oh, that it could be like it is on set during filming. "Cut! Let's take that again."

So yes, regrets, I've had a few.

From here, I can see how self-serious I was as a teen, and how ungenerous I was to my parents as a young woman struggling to find her own identity and break free from a life I did not want. It was definitely "All About Me!"

My mother. Yes, my mother, who, for all the neurotic behavior that pitched the two of us in a dreadful battle that extended throughout my teens, was still a lively, spunky woman. I now see myself in her. I know now she was an artistic spirited woman who left her parents in Canada in her twenties and went off to Europe to explore the world.

But she was not lucky enough to live in an era when choices of lifestyle were easier to make.

Why didn't I ask her more about all *her* experiences? How did she feel about *her* parents? What was it like to move as a newly married woman to England and bear her first child without any family nearby? And then having World War II break out a year later? And then to bear two more children during the war with bombs raining down nightly? What was it like returning to Canada fifteen years later to find all her old friends had established a position in Toronto society that she had not?

And my father. I was so busy being full of teenage angst, rebellion, and self-absorption that I never made an effort to know my father better. I saw a man worn down by the constant drama between my mother and me.

Why didn't I have him tell me more tales of his life at Cambridge in the 1920s? Why didn't I ask him if he missed his younger brother, who went to Bombay to live and work as a teacher, never to return?

Why didn't I ask him more about his mother, for whom I was named and whose dress I wore at my wedding? Why didn't I have more understanding that his moving to Canada at age forty or so and having to retake all his medical exams to get a license to practice medicine and get a job was blindingly stressful?

I lost both my parents by the time I was forty. Now I wish I could have an adult-to-adult relationship with them. I wish I could do a mother-daughter trip somewhere and explore all aspects of my mother and me, having fun, and seeing a new part of the world together. But the chance is gone, and I have moments of sadness about what I could have learned and enjoyed if there had been conversations between two adult humans who had forgiven each other, freed of history and baggage.

After Dominic died, of course, there were regrets! I wish I had been more openly demonstrative and affectionate. He needed it, and yet it was hard for me to give. Why? Could I have tried harder? Could I have been more like him and less like myself? Could I have expressed more belief in him and given him the confidence he needed sometimes? Could I have said "I love you" more often? We didn't say it often to each other, and certainly not in the casual way most people say it at the end of a phone call, or going out the door for one's daily errands.

What is worse? Traumatic and sudden loss? When you don't have time to say not only the goodbyes but all the "I'm sorry"s that exist, even in a perfect marriage? Or the slow and devastating path towards death when you see your partner slowly fade away, and quite possibly in pain? Do you say the difficult things, or do you try to "stay strong"?

But after losing someone, you can only burden your friends with talking about your doubts and regrets for so long. Not everyone can tolerate the psychological mess of your anguish ad infinitum.

What else gives me pause? Perhaps I did not reach the pinnacle of each of my careers. Oh, I did well and I am proud, but some of the experiences that come to only the very best were beyond my reach.

I am sad sometimes that my ballet career was just a tantalizing taste of dancing ballet on a professional stage. Dancing professionally at age fifteen, retired at sixteen, due to my sprouting up two inches. A brief career, indeed!

I wish I had been able to dance the role of Odette to the music of Tchaikovsky in the Act 2 Pas de Deux of Swan Lake. What would it have been like to be on that moonlit stage, in the magical forest by the lake, my swans nearby, and feel the strength of my prince as I leaned back against him and laid my feather-cradled head on his shoulder? To feel him lift me in the air as if I weighed next to nothing and set me down so lightly that I don't know when my feet touch the stage as the violin soars to the highest, quietest, and most exquisite note. Sigh.

In the safe space of semi-darkness of the stage, you know your body can express whatever is inside you to the fullest extent. There is such privacy and protection when you are on stage, a safe space where you can be, behave, and express without worrying about criticism or rejection. You can be someone else, or a fully expressed version of yourself, hiding within the character you're playing.

And then there's Broadway. I performed in three new shows on Broadway in the 1960s, a golden era with all the greats like Sondheim, Abbott, and Jules Stein creating at their peak. I worked directly with all of them! What an amazing time and what extraordinary memories. But I never played a leading role.

Would I have liked to dance the role of Cassie in *The Chorus Line*? Oh, my yes! Yes. When I saw Ann Reinking in the film of the same name descend the stairs in a red leotard exactly like the one I used to wear to Broadway auditions, I was green with envy. Absolutely green!

The Swan Lake pas de deux I longed to dance.
The dancers are Iana Salenko and Marian Walter of the State Ballet Berlin.
Photo credit: Carola Hoelting.

I regret that I didn't get further as a film actress. I know there were roles for me if I could have hung on a little longer into my forties. I had been told by a wise casting director many years earlier that I would never be an ingenue and that it would be much later that I'd find success when I would "grow into my roles". In Los Angeles, as I auditioned over and over again, I was coming into my mid-thirties and very unclear about who I was, but I believe in my forties I would have inhabited my "type' better at a time when more and more stories were being told about women. I would have played lawyers and doctors, serious and strong women on shows like *The Good Wife* and *Grey's Anatomy*. I was not quite a character actor, but not quite photogenic enough to be the leading lady. Could I have made it? I'll never know.

My costume design career was, by all accounts, quite successful. I was nominated three times for a "Best Costume Design" Emmy and never had a single season without a show from my start in 1985 with *The Facts of Life* to my LA exit in 2008 from *Passions*. That's quite a record, and one I am proud of.

Would I have liked to have had a break-out smash hit to design like *Friends*, or a drama like *Succession*? Of course. Emmys, please.

I have been lucky enough to see actors of mine transformed by my costumes. I've known the joy of an actor saying to me, "I really didn't feel the character until I put on this suit," or "put on this hat." That has been very gratifying. But let's agree, I never did the A-list films that were up for Oscars every year. Nevertheless, I have rehearsed my Oscar acceptance speech a million times.

Does this sound like I am disappointed in myself or self-aggrandizing into something more than I really qualify for? No, I am proud of my history, but that doesn't stop me from wishing I accomplished more. I was always one to want more. But the goal now is to get to know and accept myself, warts and all.

The funny thing is, when I have played the game "what do you want written on your tombstone" (and I do *not* want a tombstone), it's never "Here Lies a Brilliant Oscar-Winning Dancer/Actress/Designer". I think I would prefer "Here Lies Diana: She was Always Fun to be Around."

CHAPTER 34
AWOKS; I Broke The Chain

We are all a link in the endless chain from the first humans to present humans to future humans. I have broken that chain. We are a group of human beings who have ended the ancestral chain down from our forefathers and mothers and into the future. It ends with us. There is an existential aloneness I feel as a childless woman.

I used to think I was a rarity in being an older widow with no children. But research proves me wrong. According to the US Census, of the 92.2 million adults ages 55 and older in 2018, 15.2 million (16.5%) are childless, defined here as having no biological children. We are actually quite a large group.

Experts on geriatrics call us "solo agers." And the acronym AWOK means Aging Without Kids. I coined us SONKS—Single Oldsters, No Kids. But no matter what we are calling ourselves, we are here and have to learn to manage our passage from independence to dependence ourselves, which we can do. Of course, in darker moments, I wonder, "Who will come to my funeral? Who will remember me?" But that's another story. I always did like lots of attention!

We may be an only child or a member of a group of siblings, with parents, grandparents, and great-grandparents going *back*, but we have not populated our families going *forward*, and thus have no built-in self-supporting communities.

I've had to rethink my concept of family. I consider my family to be made up of people I'm related to, but also chosen family, those friends, the good and lasting friends you can depend on, and those in the community I have chosen to live in. They are my family of the heart

Why did I not have children? Am I childless by choice, chance, or circumstance?

It could be a combination of a lack of interest, combined with the circumstances of my life. In fact, when I was young, I did not fantasize about having babies. I preferred stuffed animals to dolls. I loved my rabbit and my koala bear. I never thought I wanted children, not in any real sense. I am not a person who likes giving up what I love doing, and I don't think I could have been unselfish enough to raise kids. I can't remember having that strong maternal pull that made me feel that having a child was a necessary part of my development as a loving human being.

In fact, the idea rather terrified me!

From a very young age, I thought of children as very fragile. Being born into wartime in England, where the evidence of war could not be avoided, I knew kids were being killed nearby in the nightly bombing raids. Or that they died of scarlet fever and smallpox. My mother rushed a very young, ill patient of my father's to the hospital, but the child died on the way. I was in the car with them at the time.

For years, I thought that the reason Noah invited *two* of every animal onto his ark was in case one died! But such was my world view at the time, even as a little one. Future generations of elephants and giraffes never entered my mind.

Yes, babies have scared me in the past. One day, when I was well into my twenties, I was visiting Toronto to see my sister's firstborn, Amelia. Carol had a quick doctor's check-up and asked if I would watch Amelia for an hour or so.

"It's easy," she said. "When she wakes up around 2 p.m., just give her her bottle."

Sure enough, a little after two, I heard the sound of stirring. I got the bottle and went in, but the stirring noises turned into little whimpers, then cries, which then became louder. Then they became screams of deafening proportion. I watched aghast as her little face turned purple, and I panicked. I was in sheer terror! This little niece of mine is going to scream herself to death, and then what would I tell my sister? I ran to the phone and called my father. Thankfully, he was home. By now, I was sobbing. "Amelia can't catch her br- br-breath," I sobbed, "and I don't know wh-what to do!"

My father, a doctor, chuckled. "Well, I can hear her from here, so I know she is alive and well.". At this point, my sister returned to find her older sibling a wet mess with a runny nose and face covered with tears. I never agreed to babysit again.

In Canada, I remember at age sixteen watching the movie James

Mitchener's *Hawaii* with Julie Andrews. There was a scene where Andrews' character, Jerusha, gives birth. She portrayed the agony of the experience with such ferocity and blood-curdling screams that I was horrified. The agonizing pain associated with childbirth made such an impression on me that I couldn't imagine why *anyone*, if they knew ahead of time what was coming, would endure this horrible experience!

When I left Toronto, a month into my twenty-first year, I think I knew I was never going back. In that flight towards a life in the arts on Broadway and later in Hollywood, I was rejecting a life that I would probably have had in Toronto, a certain following of the culture and lifestyle I had been brought up with, including a husband and children..

In New York in the 1960s, I was busy dancing on Broadway and having a wonderful time, staying up until all hours of the night doing the twist at Chubby Checker's club, and mixing with the Broadway stars at Downey's Bar and Grill. I certainly was not thinking in the least of replicating myself. During the same period, all my school and college friends were getting married and starting their families. One close friend said she planned to have four children by the time she was thirty, and she accomplished that. I missed out on all the baby announcements and baby showers, and all the activities associated with young families, but quite honestly, I thought my life was far more exciting.

In the 1970s, I was in Los Angeles and living the life my mother's generation couldn't even imagine. I had choices. Freedom. Pot. Plenty of sex with different partners. I did not have to conform to any given set of expectations. However, I was still trying to find out who I was, and far too busy having unproductive relationships with narcissistic actors and alcoholics to even consider becoming pregnant.

And if I had become pregnant? What if I were to hate changing diapers, watching cartoons, going to kids' school plays, and having noise *all* the time? What if kids worried me to death with high fevers, broken bones, getting lost at the mall? What if I don't want to go to soccer practice *Every Single Weekend*? (My dear friend Elinor, a ballerina, had two boys and spent hours and hours freezing in cold ice rinks as her boys played ice hockey.) And what if the kids hated me, the way I hated my mother for a few years during the Terrible Teens? Could I survive that? Could I have fulfilled the unspoken promise to a child that "I will protect you at all costs to myself and put your needs before mine?"

In the book *Selfish, Shallow and Self-Absorbed: Sixteen Writers on the Decision Not to Have Kids*, editor Meghan Daum suggests that *some* women, by their very nature, are not well-suited to what children bring to one's life, and that is okay. I am eager to absorb this as I sometimes wondered if I am not normal, if lacking the maternal urge means I am less. Am I such an outlier?

Children and grandchildren, I have discovered, engender a lot of activities for my friends. When I am in a group of women and the conversation turns to the kids and grandkids, I hear about many trips to be present for weddings, births, birthdays and graduations. Photos (mostly on iPhones these days) are passed around for admiration and approval. Do I feel left out or sad? Not really, but I do feel *different*. I am lucky that I was born in an era where I had the freedom to have or not have children. Of the 92.2 million adults ages 55 and older in 2018, 15.2 million (16.5%) are childless, having no biological children. So, I did not suffer the slings and arrows of disappointed parents, aching to be grandparents.

Time went on, and none of my relationships would be considered sensible or future-advisable. No Baby-Daddy candidates at all.

Then, at age forty, I met Dominic, the most unlikely candidate of all. He worked days as a truck driver for a movie studio transportation company, and played rock and roll with his band until all hours at the local LA clubs such as The Troubadour and Whiskey a Go Go. Gorgeous and much younger than me, we never thought our relationship would last, but it did… for thirty-five years! We never entertained one thought about raising babies. Some might say we were totally involved in self-aggrandizing careers and indulging in hedonistic lifestyles of travel and recreation. But I feel no guilt about not adding to the world's population. I'll let others do that. It's more important for babies to be wanted than just be born.

I have noticed that my friends without children seem less afraid of death. There is no wanting to live longer and longer just to keep an eye on the offspring and their offspring. Wanting to see one more marriage, one more birth. No children to leave bereft. Or not. More than one childless friend has said to me that when it comes time, they will just "head on out to the ice floe and be fine with that." I understand those feelings. In some ways, it is very freeing.

Now, in my eighties, I find myself suddenly wishing that I had some children. Not babies, not toddlers, God knows, and *certainly not teenagers*! Adult adults. Just lovely, mature, well-adjusted, successful, adult children. Wouldn't that be great? I don't care how many and they don't need to have grandchildren, but they should be somewhere in their thirties or forties, successful in their careers, but even more importantly, successful as people, good, kind, fully-formed people with the right set of values and ethics and morals, and with a great sense of humor. And I am lucky enough to find many of those qualities in my nieces and nephews.

I have also formed "chosen families," and have a number of young women (and one young man) whom I love dearly. I used to call them my surrogate daughters, and then my adopted daughters, but both those descriptions came with misunderstandings. So now I just call them my bonus daughter or my chosen daughters. I have two very special nieces (one from my sister, one from my brother), my costuming protégés Amber and Marta, dear Antonina who found me all the way from Belarus, my lovely Olivia who saved me when I was in grief over losing Dominic, Marisa, whom I have known since she was born to Dominic's closest friend, Dinah and Lauren, and Christina, my newest ballerina daughter. Christina came into my life through a Facebook exchange, and I ended up creating her wedding gown out of her mother's 1980s bridal dress. Now I never miss seeing her dance in the Nevada Ballet company's season.

When I ask people what their greatest accomplishments are, they invariably say, "My children." I bet even Jack the Ripper's mother would have said the same thing, "Such a sweet boy." But my identity has never been that of a mother. A mentor, a nurturer, perhaps.

Who will I be after I'm gone? I think there is a certain amount of ego in all of us that makes us want to be remembered, to have somehow mattered, even though we will be totally forgotten in one or two generations. Truly. No statue. We fear being insignificant even after death. Did I matter? Can I really prepare to be forgotten?

Perhaps even this book, though it will be quickly lost among the billions of published books, will have caused someone to smile, to consider something differently, to be inspired to travel, or to not be so afraid of what is ahead in old age. I may never know if I have touched anyone or had any effect, but just knowing that it is possible is a reward.

Without children, I think my legacy will be what my readers and my students remember of me. Perhaps not consciously, but if I have entered their consciousness awareness in any way, I am there to stay. One student says she often hears me in her ear when she is making a difficult costume design decision. Another student came up to me a year after I had critiqued her in a filmed scene, and I had told her that she was "totally adorable on screen". As an extra-large young woman, her eyes filled with tears as she told me she felt she had finally been *seen,* and that helped her in her confidence as an actress.

There may be more lives I have touched without even knowing it. What doors might I have opened for someone? When I was in the midst of my own career, my attention was very much focused on myself and my needs to succeed. Now, as I am closer to the end, I am more conscious of the effects of kindness, encouragement, as well as the wisdom I may impart to anyone I encounter.

My students. They are my legacy. They are my children who hopefully will remember something I once said. When a student writes something like this about me, I know I have made a difference in someone's life.

"(Diana's) passion for the art of costume design radiates through the classroom in a way that inspires you to work harder and be better. Professor Eden, she taught me so much about not only the kind of artist I wanted to be but the kind of person I wanted to be as well. Having her as a professor and a mentor gave me a newfound confidence in my craft and myself. (Her) Class solidified my decision to pursue a career in Costume Design, and I credit her with all my skills and future success in the industry. Her ability to reach students, even the more reserved ones like me, is undeniable. She pushed me to be better and come out of my shell, and in turn, I discovered my biggest passion in life." Genevive Rutter

When I am gone, and they are doing well in their costume designing careers, they will hear me in the back of their heads, whispering, "Make the bold choice, you can do it."

CHAPTER 35
THIS IS EIGHTY-FIVE

On May 12th, 2025, I turned eighty-five years of age.

Three days later, I left for a ten-day trip to Portugal with my sister and four friends. Portugal was the last place in Europe on my wish-list, and so I put together a two-city trip for us. As I did more research on the country, I discovered I had chosen two cities (Lisbon and Porto) renowned for being built on hills. It probably wasn't the wisest choice for an octogenarian with breathing troubles and a lack of stamina.

Our first apartment in Lisbon was indeed on a steep incline, and no matter whether you turned right or left upon exiting the building, you had an up or down challenge. I had also made a serious mistake in booking the apartment and not reading the fine print. It clearly stated that the apartment was on the third floor of an old building with *no elevator*! And yet, it was all doable, and the challenges seemed not terribly important. We got the concierge to assist with getting our luggage up the three floors. I got used to climbing two flights and then resting for sixty seconds before doing the final flight. We walked *downhill* to some charming cafes near us. And Uber turned out to be remarkably reasonable for our upward return trips home.

There were many steps and cobblestones in the old areas of town that could have spelled disaster, but I have now become very careful in all these situations. Whereas before I would have been gazing upward at the brightly painted buildings and the scarlet geraniums spilling over wrought-iron balconies, now I focus my eyes downward to the multitude of corners and curbs just waiting to trip me up. In fact, I cling to stair railings and creep down steps like some 109-year-old coming down the outside stairs of the Eiffel Tower. I don't care. I just want to return in one piece.

My sister Carol and I enjoy a sunset cruise in Porto, Portugal

I return to the theory that travel is still possible for us eighty-five-year-olds if you keep in mind two things: mobility and stamina. I will never again fly a fifteen-hour journey in one fell swoop. I will always stop halfway and stay overnight. I will request a wheelchair if the airport's gates are miles apart. And I will not sign up for walking tours or visits to castles or palaces that force one to stand with crowds in long lines and inch through historic rooms with no place to sit down. I have no compunction about quitting a tour halfway through when I have had enough and taking an Uber home or staying in the tour bus or van while the rest go on for yet another walkabout.

I am not embarrassed to pace myself. I care not what anyone thinks of my numerous naps. In fact, one of the benefits of being eighty-five is that you can own the limits of your body without the necessity of bravado. Nobody thinks it weird if you say you are tired!

As for how I feel at eighty-five? I, like so many others whose accounts I have been reading recently, find three things become most evident.

1. I mourn the loss of friends who've departed before me. They should not have done that.
2. I acknowledge with some irony that parts of my body hurt and there's not a whole hell of a lot I can do about it.
3. I am much more self-accepting of my limitations, and more forgiving of my shortcomings. These days, it's a good feeling to be able to sink into my true self, warts and all, without the struggle to be something more. I am more empathetic to others, less judgmental. I worry less about the small stuff.

Do I feel old for my age, or young for my age? That question assumes there is a "typical" eighty-five-year-old that we can all measure ourselves by. Everyone ages differently, and some are blessed with better heath than others, or have benefitted from life's opportunities more than others. And there are inherited genes from our parents, and a bit of luck thrown in.

I am still driving, thank goodness! Driving represents freedom and independence, and I just can't imagine wanting to go somewhere and not being able to get myself there under my own steam. I fully expect to be one stubborn and cranky old woman to the poor person who tries to take my car keys away.

What other nods to my eighty-five-year-old status have I given? I am considering installing railings leading into my swimming pool and jacuzzi. I may put two grab bars in my bathroom, one in the shower and one in the toilet. I'd rather do it now than wait until after a little slip when its necessity becomes more obvious. I can still get out of my beloved bathtub, but I hang on for dear life.

I continue my once-a-week Chair Yoga class. Anything that keeps me limber, but also as strong as I can be, will aid in balance. Yes, I can still get up from the floor without using my hands! And I swim every day during the summer, where I do upper and lower body strength exercises. No, I'm no Michael Phelps, and I can't do more than a few laps. But I am a world-class floater on my inflatable water hammock.

Though I don't wear my glasses around the house (they are either for distance and driving or for close-up), I keep a number of versions of them nearby. And I *never, ever,* drive without them.

When my short-term memory lets me down and I can't remember the name of the movie I saw on TV just last night, I don't Google it. I force my little brain neurons to go search for the name. Sometimes it takes a while.

I try to eat healthily and weigh myself every morning. But I also eat ice cream whenever the opportunity presents itself.

I also climb the one flight of stairs to my second floor, where my sewing workroom is. It's a bit harder, but if I can climb stairs in Portugal, I can climb them in my own home.

My hair is still red, I still put on makeup before going out, and I still dress in a colorful and slightly weird way. You can always see me coming.

I could have three more years, or thirteen, but it is out of my control. So, I am living in the moment and appreciating the sunshine, my friends and family, and the few things I can control, like how many frozen yogurt bars I eat in a week.

CHAPTER 36
DEATH, IT'S OK TO TALK ABOUT IT

Death! "Oh, my god!" one friend cried when I mentioned a possible title for this book, "You can't use the word death in the title! No one will buy the book." They will set my book down hurriedly like an unwieldy chunk of ice, only to pick up a good beach read, full of sex and fun and intrigue.

But it's OK to talk about death! Honestly, I am not scared of it. The slow lead-up to it, maybe. But not death itself.

Death was never that real to me until I started approaching eighty and started to consider it might actually happen. To me, I mean. I lost two close friends from college days many years earlier, one in Australia to pancreatic cancer, one in Portland to a rare brain disease. I attended neither funeral.

And, of course, my husband.

Now I am starting to lose more friends who are my contemporaries. It seems that every week another of my costume colleagues passes away, and when I check the cast list of the Broadway shows I appeared in, many of the cast members are long gone. It's like a continual "In Memoriam" reel at the Oscars. "Oh no, not him. Oh dear, her too?"

One reason for death not seeming very real was that I lost both parents, at different times, when I was away and unable to attend their funerals and burial. When my mother died, I was taking a seven-day raft trip down the Colorado River, starting at the base of the Grand Canyon. This was long before cell phones, and it wasn't until I got home to LA and called home that my dad broke the news to me. I asked if I should come home, and Dad said, "No need, everything is over now." He was exhausted, but I had no chance to come home to deal with her loss, no closure.

Similarly, I was on tour with Diana Ross, about to attend to the star in her opening night performance in Wembley Arena in London, when I got a call backstage in the stage manager's office, a chilling occurrence no matter what. It was my brother telling me that Dad had had a fatal stroke during lunchtime at his retirement home and that the funeral was tomorrow. They had had a hard time locating me. I had to stuff my feelings down inside as I only had thirty minutes to get them under control and give my full attention to my diva, my boss, and her many costume changes. I knew my dad well enough to know he would not have approved of my breaking down and failing in my obligations to other people. Stiff Upper Lip was never more apt!

Death became real for the first time for those two minutes when I stood by Dominic's body in the Emergency Room. It was so real, and yet so unreal for me that my brain could not grasp the enormity of it, the reality of it.

No, I don't want to be the last one standing. I don't want to live to be one hundred. I want to be *happy to one hundred* if I am to live that long. Content perhaps? At peace? This emphasis on longevity seems to come these days without a qualifier, with every new health tip suggesting it will prolong your life. But if life itself is painful, lonely, and miserable, why the insistence on prolonging it?

Western medicine is very focused on fixing things and, as their Hippocratic oath insists, to "do no harm." But there *is* harm, in my opinion, in constantly fixing things and extending a life that doesn't have much joy for the human in question.

I have witnessed people around my age getting cancer or other terminal illnesses and going through a couple of *years* of chemo, radiation, nausea, fatigue, losing hair, all to give them a few more years. I'd rather have the years I have left be fulfilling and let the cancers do what they may.

I am not a person who ascribes to formal religions, and I never understood the idea of going to Heaven. Maybe Heaven (or the place beyond, if there is one) is just like Home. In that case, I will look forward to going.

Recently, I have recurring dreams that I am burdened down with costumes (having shopped for a film or TV series) and don't have a car (either I can't find where I parked or it's broken) and I can't walk all the way up the hill to my house. I can't find a taxi and can't call an Uber as I can't find the link on my phone! Sometimes I get the Uber, but it can't find my house up in the hills. I am desperate to get home, to arrive at the end of that last leg. Sound familiar?

So what is "home"? So many things.

Home is rest.

Home is safety.

Home is warm. And having abundant sunshine.

Home is my surroundings, decorated the way I like it

Home is texting my sister every night

Home is my cat cuddling next to me

Home is peace—freedom from worry about anything and everything—money, war, politics, losing my marbles...

Home is freedom from my back pain

Home is... my death? If Heaven is all these things, why would I be afraid of it? Home/Heaven is the absence of all things that hurt in the real world, hurt physically, and hurt emotionally. I think the term "Rest in Peace" sounds very nice.

My mind is literal. It can't seem to deal with the abstract that is required for spiritual belief. For instance, where do we go after we die? We know where we come from. Many years ago, a sperm met an egg inside my mother and decided to get together and produce me, and after nine months, I entered the world through my mother's birth canal into the arms of the waiting human, in my case, an English midwife. Boom, I was here, but when I die, where do I go?

Do I go anywhere, and if I do go somewhere, is it a kind of a heaven? Who will be there?

I hope I can also visit the part of heaven where the Rainbow Bridge exists. Bless the person who wrote that poem so that we can all visualize our beloved pets having a grand time running and jumping and chasing balls and sniffing each other and being happy. I'd love to see Pax again, our cocker spaniel from growing up, and then my very first cat that I got on Broadway during "A Funny Thing Happened on the Way to the Forum," my Tigger, who, sadly, fell to an untimely death from my fourth-floor window when I was away on tour. And Greta, fluffy angora Greta, whose white hair was everywhere. And then Dominic's and my first adopted cat sisters from the same litter, Gwendolyn and Cecily, who were named after the characters in "The Odd Couple." And then a brief time with Pierre, whom we called Lucky Pierre because we rescued him from the pound. He proved to be not quite so lucky when a huge owl caught him. And then our second set of girl cats, Sophia and Gina, named after the Italian movie stars, and of course, Nala, who is still with me.

And my parents. Even with all that went wrong during certain periods, I would love to see them again. Will they look like they looked the last time they visited me in LA, looking slightly older than I remembered, and a wee bit eccentric? Or will they look like they looked in the photo I have of them on Windmill Point in Muskoka, my mother with a cigarette dangling from her fingers, both looking happy?

My Mum and Dad looking relaxed, around 1952.

I dearly hope Dominic will be there, smiling, and waiting to greet me as he used to by the luggage carousel at the airport when I came back from a trip. Will he be young and gorgeous and looking at me with those dark eyes and beautiful eyelashes? Or will he be 62? the age when he died, still handsome but with salt and pepper hair and a thickening waist? Will he still be mad at me for not keeping the refrigerator organized the way he liked it?

I do want to see them all, but will I go to Heaven?

No, I tend to think my ashes and my energies just go back into the vault of the universe, the great complex of molecules that make up the world, to be recycled into new plants, beings, and energies.

So, where do I want my ashes to go? Foolishly, since I won't be around to care, I'd like to control where they go. Not into the cold earth. They can go into water, but not the ocean, once again too cold. I wouldn't mind the warm waters of the Caribbean. But I also fancy my ashes going into the desert. If my ashes, if my DNA can fix itself to another, and become part of a new plant popping up through the rocks in the desert, that would be lovely.

So what is a good death? Did Dominic have one, falling to the ground and, I hope to believe, gone in an instant, no suffering? He died while he was still active, enriched with many, many friends who celebrated him at his exceptionally "fun" showbiz memorial.

When I hear that someone has died in their sleep, I am, in fact, quite envious. "What a way to go," I think. I'd like to go that way as long as someone finds me quickly. Finding me four or five days afterward does not fit my romantic imagining of my death.

For my good death, I have a scenario. I have chosen the day after I return from a glorious holiday, full of wonderful memories and energized by new experiences and friendships. I want to die, of course, in my home and not in a hospital. I want to lie in my bed, in the *center* of the bed as in all the famous movie scenes, surrounded by family and friends who tiptoe in and out while I am in my final hours. We will whisper loving words to each other. I will be wearing a nightgown my mother made for me in the 1970s. It's a full-length gown with sleeves, made of the softest coral silk charmeuse, and inset at the neck is a combination of tiny lace and my mother's hand embroidery. I have it to this day, and it is still in beautiful shape.

Music will be playing softly, probably Swan Lake. Maybe some scented candles will burn. And then I will quietly slip away.

"Mum?" says Nala.

"Yes, my sweetie puss, what is it?"

"Maybe you and I should go together at the same time. I will come and curl up next to you, as I always do. I will lie alongside your torso, and you can put your hand on my tummy. We will just head on over to The Bridge together."

"That sounds perfect," I say.

THE END

ACKNOWLEDGEMENTS

First, a big shout-out to my photo editor, my sister Carol Moore-Ede, who has been straightening my crooked horizons for a long time! You make the photos look so much better.

To my first writing teacher, Judith Huge, who taught me all about the story arc, thank you. You inspired me the first time and you to inspire me now. And the cats thank you too.

To my friend Linda Bergman, with whom I swapped chapters throughout 2025 for feedback and comment. I appreciate your friendship and humor, as well as all the notes and corrections of the errant comma, and my other writing ticks.

To Paula Scardamalia, my editor, whose big welcoming smile on every zoom was as important as the edits she so expertly made, thank you. Working with you was such a pleasure, and I will stop using "SO," so often.

To Judi Fennell for being so diligent in formatting the final version and educating me on the forms of publishing.

To my IWWG (International Womens' Writers Guild) sisters, for your support and the "village" you provide.

To Antonina and Michael Lerch, whose encouragement and support have known no bounds. I appreciate and love you so much.

To Amber, my researcher, former protégé, assistant, cat sitter, movie goer and friend, thank you.

And last but very much not least, my friends and neighbors who have been bugging me all year with "when is your next book coming out? I can't wait to read it". Bless you! I hope you like it.

Carol Moore-Ede Photojournalist, author,
Thinking Outside the Box: Pioneers of Canadian Modernism
Fitzhenry & Whiteside - Sutherland House Books
http://cmooreede-photojournalist.photography

IN CASE YOU MISSED IT:

My previous book, Stars in Their Underwear, tells my story from my birth in England in the midst of WW2 with nightly bombing raids above, to my Broadway career as a dancer during the glorious 1960s when I worked with Broadway greats Carol Burnett, Judy Holliday, Stephen Sondheim, Hal Prince, Zero Mostel, and more. It follows me as I move to Los Angeles in the wild 1970s to pursue my acting career, only to find myself transitioning to costume design under the mentoring eye of Bob Mackie, who hires me as his assistant. The book pulls back the curtain on the "stars" I have costumed, such as Diana Ross, Betty White, George Clooney, Tony Danza, Reba McEntire, and so many more.

Here is the prologue for you to enjoy, about Diana Ross' famous Central Park Concert in 1983.

https://www.amazon.com/Stars-Their-Underwear-unpredictable-Hollywoods-ebook/dp/B08GNZWJFG?ref_=ast_author_mpb

PROLOGUE

"Dee, Bring me my robe!"

Those five words from the lips of superstar Diana Ross battled their way through a howling wind and across a rain-drenched stage to where I was crouched near the top of the steps leading up to stage left. I was *"Dee,"* her costume coordinator, and she needed a robe to protect her from the deluge. It was 6.14 pm on July 21st, 1983, Central Park, New York and the concert she had planned for so long was about to be sabotaged by an unexpected storm of massive proportions.

She had meant for me to bring her the white, beaded, fur-trimmed wrap-around gown, but I thought the white Versace jacket would give her more protection from the cold. As I got to her at center stage, she whispered. *"No, the pretty one."*

July 21st started out hot and sunny. Diana Ross's free concert to raise money for a children's playground in the park had finally arrived after months of planning. The crew got to the venue early in the day, casually dressed in tank tops and shorts. Spirits were high as we set up the stage for dancers' rehearsals and made last-minute adjustments. Lights were still being hung overhead on the high metal scaffolding, two 24 by 34-foot video screens were being installed, microphones tested, and my wardrobe crew and I checked Miss Ross's trailer behind the stage, making sure all her costumes were ready for the big night. The concert was to be broadcast worldwide live on the Showtime cable channel, adding a heightened sense of anticipation. No going back and re-filming things if anything went wrong!

At around 2:00 pm Diana arrived, looking jaunty in tight white jeans, white t-shirt, and a baseball cap. A stickler for details and always eager for perfection, she checked every aspect of the show before doing her soundcheck. She would never admit to being nervous, but I knew from our previous conversations how important this night was to her. A large crowd started gathering on the Central Park Great Lawn as early as 1:00 pm, and the mood was festive; a beautiful mix of all ages and races, coming together with their blankets and picnic hampers, ready to enjoy their beloved Diana. The concert was free, and this was going to be a great night!

The live broadcast started right on time at 6:00 pm. A few minutes into the opening song, a strong wind came up, and Diana had a hard time keeping her hair out of her eyes or over her microphone. At first, it was only annoying. No big deal. Except, in the distance to the northeast, we saw a very dark cloud approaching fast and knew that something BIG was about to happen. There was absolutely no doubt it was heading straight for us!

Diana continued to sing in her rhinestone orange lace Bob Mackie bodysuit, her face radiant with the joy of finally getting to this moment with her fans. As she struggled against the wind, I thought how dramatic it would be if I could get her to put on her orange cape over her bodysuit. It was not much of a cape, one layer of lightweight chiffon but I could imagine it flowing out behind her like *The Winged Victory of Samothrace*. I knew well her fine-tuned sense of the dramatic. The quick-change room was right under the stage by the exit stairs, so I ran down and grabbed the cape, climbed back up and crouched at the edge of the stage, trying to get her attention. Finally, she beckoned to me to bring the cape to her.

It was a struggle to get it on as the wind was so fierce, she couldn't find the armholes, and I thought she might give up and shake me away. But a moment or two later, something clicked, and she started "working it." She transformed into a mythical goddess spirit facing down the almighty storm, the figurehead at the bow of the boat. "*Stop, in the name of love*" she sang, with her arm outstretched, palm up, as if she could 'will' the wind to stop. With the cape streaming out behind her like an insane orange flame, and the rain coming down at a 45-degree angle, lit by a single spotlight, Diana was captured by the cameras, both video and still. The iconic images would appear the next morning on the front page of the New York Times, and newspapers and magazines all over the world.

We were all drenched! I mean, really drenched. But Diana said, "It's taken me a long time to get here, I'm not going anywhere." And she didn't. She remained totally in control. The lamps were swinging wildly on the high lighting towers over the stage, and the musicians were starting to unplug their instruments as the fear of electrocution became very real. Water ran down the stairs into the quick-change room onto my surge strip where I had appliances plugged in. I was ankle-deep in mud and eventually kicked off my sandals, never to find them again. It was chaos backstage! Park officials, the mayor of New York, the fire department, and Barry Diller, president of Paramount Pictures, all were trying to get her to stop the concert out of concern for the safety of the nearly eight-hundred-thousand people in the park, who might have been injured in a stampede to get out of the rain. "It's only water," Diana told the crowd. "Walk slowly and safely out of the park." When Miss Ross felt the crowds were calm enough, she finally, and reluctantly left the stage.

She went into the comfort of her trailer, and soon after into the limo that whisked her away. Director Steve Binder and technical staff emerged from the warm dark confines of the video truck into the cold rain and seemed surprised that it was actually wet outside. The musicians left in their vans, and one by one, the stage crew could do no more and also left. But my wardrobe crew of three and I were still there.

We were gathering up what we could find of Miss Ross' costumes when suddenly, all the lights went out! There we were, in pitch black, wet, muddy Central Park.

"Hey everyone," I told my crew, "See if you can find some black garbage bags. Cut a hole for your heads and make yourselves ponchos." I encouraged them to take a sip of Miss Ross's XO Hennessy brandy (I thought she would forgive us under the circumstances) and get their sewing scissors out. We held them in front of our bodies as a meager means of self-defense.

Thus, our little band of wardrobe warriors walked out of a potentially dangerous Central Park in the pitch black. We made it to Central Park South, and then to the upscale Le Parker Meridian Hotel on 56th Street. The hotel had been told to give anyone a room who needed one, and they never looked askance at our bizarrely attired group or even at my muddy bare feet. The next morning, I ordered my usual room service breakfast, which came with a copy of the New York Times. There on the front page was Diana's photo in the orange bodysuit, face soaked but defiant, orange cape streaming out behind her. I called her immediately, and she had not seen the paper. But she had already announced to the crowd the night before that "we will do the show again tomorrow," and the city, after many meetings late into the night, had finally no choice but to agree. Diana asked me to drive out to her house in Greenwich, Connecticut, and gather up some new costumes from her storage room. I brought back the fuchsia sequin bodysuit, which looked like a super-shiny second skin on her, the fuchsia tulle wrap, some fresh dry shoes, and a backup choice of gowns.

It was another lovely sunny day, but this time no storm on the horizon. Everyone was elated at the return of the thousands and thousands of fans, and the concert was brilliant. We all felt we had been a part of history. Who knew, after many years, that maybe we were. But my story started long before that, on another continent, where a storm of a different sort was under way.

ABOUT THE AUTHOR

Diana Eden is a three-time Emmy nominee for her costume design work in Hollywood. She designed numerous prime-time television series, movies, pilots, as well as stage productions in Los Angeles and New York.

Her so-called retirement and move in 2008 to Las Vegas brought her more costume design for films and stage shows in "the entertainment capital of the world", a professorship at UNLV (University of Nevada, Las Vegas) teaching tomorrow's filmmakers about costume for film, and a writing career that includes contributing nearly forty articles for Travel Over 80 section of Journeywoman.com, plus the publication of her first memoir *Stars in Their Underwear: My Unpredictable Journey from Broadway Dancer to Costume Designer for some of Hollywood's Biggest Stars*. in 2020.

In her new book "GETTING OLD AND OTHER INDIGNITIES: A Memoir of Aging with Adventure and Style," she explores her seventh decade while working in Las Vegas, grieving the loss of her husband of 35 years, and her eighties as she continues to travel, write, teach, and get (just a little) old!